WILLIA...

WILLIAM MORRIS

Selected Poems

edited with an introduction by
Peter Faulkner

Fyfield Books

First published in 1992 by
Carcanet Press Limited
208-212 Corn Exchange Buildings
Manchester M4 3BQ

A CIP catalogue record for this book is available
from the British Library
ISBN 0 85635 926 2

The Publisher acknowledges financial assistance
from the Arts Council of Great Britain

Typeset in 10pt Palatino by Bryan Williamson, Darwen
Printed and bound in England by SRP Ltd, Exeter

Contents

Introduction

William Morris (1834-1896) was a great Victorian of prodigious talents; so he has several reputations. To the general public today he is best known as a pattern designer – the popularity of 'Morris patterns' as currently marketed in numerous forms from curtain fabrics to wrapping-paper attests to this. To those interested in social and cultural criticism, on the other hand, he is the earliest and perhaps still the most significant English Marxist, as evoked by E.P. Thompson in his fine biography subtitled 'From Romantic to Revolutionary'. To bibliophiles and typographers, he is the founder of the Kelmscott Press. But in his own lifetime he was very well known as a poet, one of the second generation of Victorian poets along with Dante Gabriel Rossetti, Christina Rossetti, and Swinburne; only his political commitment, it is said, prevented him from succeeding Tennyson as Poet Laureate when the latter died in 1892. (England still awaits a Socialist Poet Laureate.)

He published six volumes of poetry: *The Defence of Guenevere* (1858); *The Life and Death of Jason* (1867); *The Earthly Paradise* (1868-70), his most popular poem; *Love is Enough* (1873); *Sigurd the Volsung* (1876); and *Poems by the Way* (1891). *Jason*, *The Earthly Paradise* and *Sigurd* are long narrative poems, and *Love is Enough* a complicated poetic morality play. These works cannot be fully represented in a selection like the present one, which necessarily concentrates on the shorter poems, and presents them in chronological order. In general the reader will find that these shorter poems may be divided roughly into two modes, the dramatic and the lyrical, which we might associate respectively with the two major poets of the previous generation, Browning and Tennyson. The first volume is largely dramatic, drawing much of its material from the Middle Ages. But the shorter poems of the period 1867-73 are more lyrical and indeed personal, although it is important to remember that a poet using the pronoun 'I' is not necessarily writing an autobiography. The roughness and force of the early poetry is replaced by a much more fluent and elegant movement. However, Morris came to see in this a danger of losing poetic force altogether, and he then went to Northern, particularly Icelandic, sources for a renewal of energy. He wrote less original poetry in the last twenty years of his life – although finding time to translate *The Aeneid*, *The Odyssey* and *Beowulf* – but this included some of the first Socialist verse to be published in England. Altogether it is a varied and interesting achievement, and the modern reader can find much to enjoy both in following Morris from his youthful Romanticism to his mature commitment, and in the varied qualities of drama and lyricism in the poems read individually.

Morris was born in comfortable financial circumstances in Walthamstow in 1834, the son of a successful businessman. He was educated at Marlborough College, where he developed a great interest in the English past, and went up to Exeter College, Oxford in 1853. He was influenced by the High Church movement and intended to enter the Church, but at Oxford he developed an interest in architecture and other forms of art, meeting his lifelong friend Edward Burne-Jones. He started to write poetry, surprising his friends by his facility in the art. When he left the university in 1856, Morris entered the architectural practice of G.E. Street, but on moving to London he and Burne-Jones fell under the spell of the charismatic Pre-Raphaelite painter and poet, Dante Gabriel Rossetti, who encouraged them both to paint; Morris showed more talent for pattern design than for figure composition. Rossetti led a group of young artists back to Oxford to decorate the new debating hall of the Oxford Union, though their efforts soon faded away due to the defective technique employed. Here at Oxford Morris met the striking Jane Burden, whom he was to marry in 1860, and whose features, often painted by Rossetti, have become one of the best-known Pre-Raphaelite icons.

Meanwhile, in 1858, Morris published a volume of poetry entitled *The Defence of Guenevere and Other Poems*. The poems from that volume included a number on Arthurian themes, like the title poem. Interest in the Arthurian legends developed greatly in the early nineteenth century, following the re-publication of

8

Malory's *Morte D'Arthur* in 1816. Tennyson's lifelong interest produced 'The Lady of Shalott' (1832), 'Morte D'Arthur' (1842) and 'Sir Galahad' (1842), leading to the first series of *Idylls of the King* in 1859, and the completion of the work in twelve books in 1882. Many other writers and painters employed Arthurian subject-matter, which seems to have a particular appeal to the Victorians, aware of living in a period of unprecedented social and cultural change. Perhaps there was some stability in the medieval past which might offer guidance, or at least relaxation, in a bewildering modern world. For Morris, certainly, the medieval period was of compelling interest. But – and here the peculiar power of his imagination shows itself – Morris did not idealize the medieval past; nor did he use it, in the fashion of the later Tennyson, to read a lesson to his contemporaries. He preferred to emphasize its dramatic qualities.

The two Arthurian poems included here both show this dramatic power. In 'The Defence of Guenevere' we are given a vivid account of the queen defending herself with reckless courage against those accusing her of adultery. Her primary stance is of defiance, and we are led by our closeness to Guenevere's point of view (a remarkable achievement for a young male poet) to admire her courage. Yet the question of her guilt remains. Unlike Tennyson in 'Guinevere', Morris offers no explicit moral judgment, and the reader is left uneasily divided between respect and dubiety. The following poem, 'King Arthur's Tomb', offers a different perspective. It dramatizes Lancelot's journey to Glastonbury after the death of Arthur and Guenevere's entering the nunnery of which she became abbess. Lancelot is still full of loving memories of Guenevere. Exhausted, he lies down to rest with his head on a tomb – Arthur's, although he does not know it. Guenevere comes to Lancelot and upbraids him. The series of questions she asks expresses her bewilderment and distress over what has happened. She now sees herself as having behaved wickedly, sinfully, and finally denounces Lancelot as a 'crooked sword'. Lancelot falls, and she goes away, believing she has killed him, but still not completely able to forget. Ironically the poem ends with Lancelot awakening, remembering that he had fainted when she upbraided him, and having heard a bell. Does that bell announce Guenevere's death – the death she had looked forward to as she left Lancelot for dead? Again, the poem is not explicit, and thus engages the reader in the full complexity of the human situation so effectively dramatized in the poetry.

A similarly sombre mood pervades most of the poems in the volume, though their settings vary. A number take their origins from Morris's reading of Jean Froissart, the chronicler of the wars of the fourteenth century in France. 'Concerning Geffray Teste Noire', for instance, takes the reader vividly into that world of violence and cunning, and includes a reference to Froissart ('the Canon of Chimay'); the account of the defence of the castle of Ventadour surrounds, via the discovery of two skeletons, the constructed story of a pair of dead lovers. In these poems, as in much Romantic art, love and death are closely linked.

The three short poems 'The Wind', 'The Blue Closet' and 'The Tune of Seven Towers' take the reader into a more mysterious, if no less disturbing, world. The latter two take their origins from water-colour paintings by Rossetti which Morris owned, but the relation of poem to picture is largely atmospheric. In all three poems – which tended to arouse the contempt of conventional critics and the enthusiasm of young admirers – a narrative is hinted at, but disrupted by symbol and music. The reader finds himself in a world to whose logic he has no access, and can only respond to the intimations of romance and disaster by accepting the mood and pattern without seeking clear explanations. These poems demand to be read in terms of Keats's Negative Capability, when the reader refrains from any 'irritable striving after fact and reason',[1] and in so doing point forward to the Symbolist Movement in France later in the century.

The early poems were not well received, and the multi-talented Morris did not immediately write more. With his marriage in 1859 he became involved in domestic matters. He was wealthy enough to be able to commission a house from his architect friend Philip Webb, which he called the Red House, at Upton in Kent. But he and Jane were dissatisfied with the furnishings currently available and the poor quality of contemporary craftsmanship and design. Morris therefore persuaded a number of his friends, including Rossetti and Burne-Jones, to join him in establishing a firm to supply the market with high-quality goods, from stained glass to furniture. Thus was founded the firm which was to become Morris and Co. and for which Morris produced the enormous number of splendid and vigorous designs for many types of wares, including chintzes and wallpapers, for which he is principally known to the general public today. His energetic involvement in the firm, and the birth of two daughters in these years, must have left little time for writing. Yet, having abandoned a planned series of poems on the fall of Troy, Morris did start writing again, publishing the highly successful *Life and Death of Jason* in 1867, retelling the classical story of Jason and the Golden Fleece, and of Medea, in a leisurely style. Within the lengthy narrative (there are seventeen books) Morris interpolated a number of lyrics. These arise naturally in their contexts, but also have an attractive lyricism which makes it possible to enjoy them separately; four are included in the present selection (see pp.80-87). All these songs have in common a sense of loss, expressed in mellifluous couplets: loss became a central theme in the middle period of Morris's writing life, when the early days of his married happiness were moving towards disillusionment and regret.

Such feelings found frequent expression in Morris's poetry in these years. *The Earthly Paradise* is pervaded by them, at least until its final volume. This very long poem is organized around the voyage of a group of fourteenth-century wanderers who eventually find themselves in 'some Western land' where they are welcomed and settle down, telling stories in alternation with their hosts for every month of the year, beginning in March. The twenty-four narrative poems thus constitute the bulk of the work. But it is also framed by an introductory 'Apology' and a concluding 'Envoi', while each month is introduced by a poem. All these are included here, together with two particularly beautiful songs from the stories (see pp.88-104). The 'Apology' contains probably Morris's most-quoted line, 'The idle singer of an empty day', and its overall defence of the ensuing poem shows what may be seen as either a decent modesty ('Of Heaven or Hell I have no power

11

to sing') or what Donald Davie was later to describe, in the case of Hardy, as 'a critical selling short of the poetic vocation'.[2] Its limited claims for the poem – or for poetry – show that for Morris, at this time at least, poetry had lost the very high status and power that it had possessed for the Romantics (whom Morris admired). Shelley had claimed in the *Defence of Poetry* in 1821 that poets were 'the unacknowledged legislators of mankind'. But for Morris here the poet is not one of the mighty men who can slay the 'ravening monsters' of bewilderment and pain that beset mankind; he can only 'build a shadowy isle of bliss' for the solace, not the salvation, of his readers. There seems to be a significant self-challenge in the question: 'Dreamer of dreams, born out of my one time, / Why should I strive to set the crooked straight?' The implied answer is to accept the self-pitying view that there is nothing to be done by the poet unfortunate enough to be born in the nineteenth century except to offer his dreams as solacing entertainment. But there remains the half-acknowledged sense that the poet should be trying to 'straighten' the 'crooked' realities of his times. Morris is not fully able to accept the limited role he ascribes to his own poetry.

Solutions to this unresolved problem might be sought in either of two directions: in some sort of non-poetic activity aimed at changing society, which Morris was later to commit himself to in Socialism; or in writing a poetry that penetrated more deeply into the bewilderment and pain and so might be held to offer a way beyond it. This, I believe, Morris achieves in a number of his short poems of this period, including the twelve three-stanza poems for each month from March to February. When J.W. Mackail was writing his authorized biography of Morris soon after his death, he refrained from trying to tell the story of the troubled years of the failure of Morris's marriage with the remark that, 'In the verses that frame *The Earthly Paradise* there is an autobiography so delicate and so outspoken that it must be left to speak for itself.' There is no need for the modern reader to be concerned with the autobiographical significance of these poems: what matters is their success in evoking a moving sense of painful experiences – similar in this to Meredith's sequence of sixteen-line 'sonnets', *Modern Love*, of 1862, though less dramatic. The poems constitute a series of meditations, rather than a narrative line, in which the poet attempts to understand his own feelings through the changing landscape. The weight of subjectivity is almost overwhelming, especially in 'November', when the poet tries to cure his introspective sickness with the call 'Look out upon the real world', only to find that the 'void patience' of nature serves to emphasize his sense of alienation: 'how can these have part, / These outstretched feverish hands, this restless heart?' In all these poems, ideas of love and beauty are threatened by the ghostly figures of Fear and Death, which the world has tried to forget. The summer poems come nearest to offering a vision of happiness, 'June' and 'August' in particular, where the English landscape is beautifully and comfortingly evoked, but even in these poems there is a sense of limitation. 'February' ends with the sense of the poet's continuing, despite all the odds, to 'hope for joy new born again' to offset the unforgettable power of memory and grief.

These sombre but moving poems are linked thematically to a number of others written at the same time (see pp.105-17), and using the same elevated, romantic register (the beloved is often addressed as 'thou'). Despite Morris's stylistic variations, the sense of loss and unhappiness is overwhelming. In this context the vigorous common sense of 'Hic' in the dialogue 'Hapless Love' is appealing – he can open out the world for us by imagining a series of disasters that have nothing to do with love. However, 'Ille' is the typical protagonist of these poems, an unhappy lover who must tell his story of unrequited love, and who prefers his own grief to the robust advice to go on his way and find 'some dainty maid / To sit with in thy chestnut shade.' Ille prefers to sit apart, nursing his love and sorrow, but the poem has asserted the possibility of a more active response. Perhaps something similar may be discerned in 'L'Envoi' to *The Earthly Paradise*, where the poet sends his book into the world, hoping that it will encounter the generous spirit of Geoffrey Chaucer (whose series of *Canterbury Tales* provided an inspiring model for Morris's poem). Chaucer will give credit for the effort 'to lay / The ghosts

13

that crowd about life's empty day', and the poet will feel satisfaction in having 'made fresh flowers spring up from hoarded seed.' Although still describing himself as the 'idle singer of an empty day', the poet can feel that his efforts were not worthless: 'No little part it was for me to play.' The poet's contribution to society is significant if limited: the singing is not altogether idle.

Morris's next publication was *Love is Enough* (1873), an elaborately structured work combining elements of lyricism and the morality play, centred on the story of King Pharamond and his search for love. Its complicated method precluded popularity, and it has only recently begun to receive much critical attention. The passages entitled 'The Music', included here, show Morris handling a complex lyrical form with much skill and elegance (see pp.118-25). The sequence ends positively: 'Cry out! for he heedeth, fair Love that led home.' Yet the reader cannot help remembering that in the sequence as a whole the pain and suffering of love have been greatly emphasized, and may feel uneasy that the figure who finally triumphs ('fair Love') is an amalgam of the spiritual and the erotic. We are not sure where to locate his power and how to understand his significance. Morris had abandoned Christianity early in life and took little interest in it; but in this poem it seems to play a covert role in supporting a case that needs to be made in more directly human terms.

Morris came to feel dissatisfied with the gently flowing narrative mode of the early *Earthly Paradise* stories, although it appealed to many readers: their point of view was well expressed by a reviewer in 1871 who introduced some slightly critical comments with the observation:

> The melody of Mr. Morris's verse is so sweet, the movement so smooth, that we care as little to assume the attitude of critics towards these poems as to analyse our feelings while we watch the light playing on calm waters beneath a cloudless summer sky.[3]

Morris turned for inspiration to the literature of the North, particularly the Icelandic sagas, which helped him to develop a more vigorous and positive manner. This can be seen in 'The Lovers of Gudrun', a poem in the final volume based on the *Laxdaela Saga*. When Swinburne wrote to praise the poem, Morris replied to express his pleasure, and went on to say that he knew that:

> the book would have done me more credit if there had been nothing in it but the Gudrun, although I don't think the others quite the worst things I have done – Yet they are all too long and flabby – damn it – [4]

Morris studied the Icelandic language with a native speaker, Eiríkr Magnússon, produced a prose version of the *Volsunga Saga* in 1870, and visited Iceland in 1871 and 1873. It was his enthusiasm for the culture of the North that led him to write his last large-scale narrative poem, *Sigurd the Volsung*, published in December 1876. This tells the story of the same hero celebrated by Wagner in *The Ring* under his German name, Siegfried, and was part of the same movement to assert the Teutonic roots of North European culture. Despite Morris's enthusiasm and the critics' approval, *Sigurd* was not popular with the reading public; there was no second edition until 1887.

This aspect of Morris's poetry is under-represented here, because *Sigurd* is not a poem from which extracts can be usefully taken, and even 'The Lovers of Gudrun' is far too long for inclusion. However, a number of shorter poems express his enthusiasm for the North. These did not appear in book form until 1891, in *Poems by the Way*, but belong to the earlier period (see pp.126-56).

'To the Muse of the North' is the earliest, 1869, and its rhyming couplets do not altogether avoid self-pity, but the poet is able to recognize and salute 'those souls of thine / Whose greatness through the tangled world doth shine.' The 'grey eyes kind and unafraid' with which the Muse is endowed suggest an admired ability to accept the realities of life without flinching but also with humanity. 'Iceland First Seen' records Morris's visit of 1871, and shows his response to a landscape very different from the England of his earlier descriptions. The poem's energy and directness of tone convey respect for an ancient culture felt to contain the seeds of a world in which 'the roses [will] spring up by thy feet

15

that the rocks of the wilderness wore.' In order to convey his response to Iceland, Morris employs a vocabulary which largely avoids Romance elements in favour of Old English, with corresponding patterns of grammar. The poem 'Gunnar's Howe above the House at Lithend', also from 1871, focuses on a particular place with legendary associations. The direct narrative names the dead hero, whose story remains alive. Gunnar embodies the true heroic spirit, 'glad-eyed without grudging or pain', and his story remains memorable after nine hundred years. But the final emphasis is on the strangeness of the place, with a dusk that darkens at dawn, and summer having to toil to bring any life to the land. In these poems we move away from introspection to an awareness of a culture which was coming to have the greatest significance for Morris.

In a letter which Morris wrote to Andreas Scheu, a refugee Austrian socialist, in 1883, he gave an account of his earlier life and explained something of his enthusiasm for works of Icelandic literature:

> the delightful freshness and independence of thought of them, the air of freedom which breathes through them, their worship of courage (the great virtue of the human race), their utter unconventionality took my heart by storm.[5]

He also remarked that his visits taught him: 'one lesson . . . that the most grinding poverty is a trifling evil compared with the inequality of classes.'[6] This remark suggests the direction that Morris's development was taking at that time – towards Radical and eventually Socialist politics. In the next decade he found himself increasingly disturbed by what Carlyle had called the Condition-of-England question, and in particular by the problem to which Ruskin had eloquently drawn attention in the second volume of *The Stones of Venice* in 1853: that of the quality of life of the industrial worker. Not only were urban living conditions often appallingly squalid, and hours of work excessively long, but the work itself was meaninglessly repetitive. The specialization of function which underpinned the Industrial Revolution vastly increased the possibilities of production, but at the cost of the worker's creativity. For a man like Morris who found much of his happiness in the use of his matchless creative energies – and in the years after 1875 he was at the height of his career as a designer for his firm – the recognition that for most men work could bring no joy (as Ruskin believed that it had to the medieval craftsman) was deeply disturbing. Morris began to search for a solution to these issues in the only place where one could be found – in politics. These were the early years of European Socialism, and in January 1883 Morris joined a small group calling itself the Democratic Federation, led by the eloquent if domineering Marxist, H.M. Hyndman. The next decade was full of political activity – in 1889 alone, for example, Morris attended sixty-three political meetings and spoke at most of them. Inevitably Morris the writer decided to devote his talents to the cause of Socialism, and he wrote for (and subsidized) two magazines, *Justice* for the Social Democratic Federation, and then the better-known *Commonweal* for the Socialist League, which began publication in February 1885. It was to *Commonweal* in 1885 that he contributed his narrative poem about the 1848 Paris Commune, *The Pilgrims of Hope*, two extracts from which are included here (see pp.134-40). Between 1884 and 1887 he also wrote the political poems published by the League as 'Chants for Socialists' (see pp.140-44).

Morris included some of his 'Chants for Socialists' in *Poems by the Way* in 1891. The volume was issued by his own, recently founded Kelmscott Press, which produced beautiful books in types designed by Morris himself – his last, and perhaps his most influential, contribution to the great upsurge of the arts and crafts in Britain at the end of the century. It is not surprising that this heterogenous collection did not attract very much attention, and it is evident that Morris no longer saw poetry as one of his central activities. The book includes uncollected poems going back to 1868; translations, mostly from the Icelandic, of 1871; some ballads of the 1870s; three extracts from *The Pilgrims of Hope*; a number of short poems for tapestry or embroidery inscriptions; and some recent ballads such as 'The Folk-Mote by the River', which neatly combines (like the earlier prose-story *A Dream of John Ball*) a tale of the late Middle Ages with a political message for Morris's own time. The victory of what is felt to be good over evil, of the people over their potential exploiter, is not easily won, and so the final effect is not facile:

> And sooth it is that the River-land
> Lacks many an autumn-gathering hand...

> And yet in the Land by the River-side
> Doth never a thrall or an Earl's man bide...

Humanity has to fight for its freedom, and this cannot be done without loss and suffering; but perhaps out of sacrifice the just society can grow. It was to the assertion of this possibility that Morris devoted the energies of his last years: in direct propaganda for the Socialist cause; in the imaginative fables of his prose romances from *The House of the Wolfings* in 1888 to the posthumously published *The Sundering Flood*; and to poems like 'The Folk-Mote' and, more succinctly, 'Mine and Thine', which expresses in its vigorous couplets all Morris's indignation at a world dominated by greed and selfishness.

Not everyone will be as moved as I am by the sentiments of 'Mine and Thine'. Some may prefer the lines Morris wrote for the embroidered valance round his bed at Kelmscott Manor, designed by his daughter May. But the man who wrote poetry in such varied modes and on such varied themes ought still to be read, and I hope that this volume will encourage that activity.

Notes

1 Keats to George and Thomas Keats, 22 Dec. 1817, in M. Buxton Forman (ed.), *The Letters of John Keats* (1952), 71.
2 Donald Davie, *Thomas Hardy and British Poetry* (1973), 40.
3 G.W. Cox, unsigned review in *Edinburgh Review*, Vol.133 (Jan. 1871), 244; in P. Faulkner (ed.), *William Morris. The Critical Heritage* (1973), 125.
4 Morris to Swinburne, 21 Dec. 1869; in N. Kelvin (ed.), *The Collected Letters of William Morris*, Vol.I (1984), 100.
5 Morris to Scheu, 15 Sept. 1883, in ibid., Vol.II (1987), 229.
6 Ibid.

Suggested Reading

The fullest discussion of Morris's poetry is by:
J.M.S. Tompkins, *William Morris. An Approach to the Poetry*, 1988.

Reviews published in Morris's lifetime may be found in:
P. Faulkner, editor, *William Morris. The Critical Heritage*, 1973.

The poetry is also discussed in:
E.P. Thompson, *William Morris: Romantic to Revolutionary*, 1955; revised edition, 1977.
Philip Henderson, *William Morris. His Life, Work and Friends*, 1967.
Paul Thompson, *The Work of William Morris*, 1967.
Jack Lindsay, *William Morris. His Life and Work*, 1975.
The Morris number of *Victorian Poetry*, Vol.XIII, Nos. 3-4, Fall-Winter, 1975.

The Text

The poems in this volume are taken from *The Collected Works of William Morris*, edited by May Morris, 1910-1915.

This volume contains some of Morris's most energetic and dramatic poems, but it was not well received by the reviewers at the time. It was seen as Pre-Raphaelite at a time when Pre-Raphaelitism was still uncomfortably radical: it lacked the elegance admired in early Tennyson. The poems may be divided into three main groups, Arthurian, Froissartian and 'atmospheric', and are printed in that order. The Arthurian mode is seen in 'The Defence of Guenevere' and 'King Arthur's Tomb', the Froissartian in 'Concerning Geffray Teste Noire', 'The Judgment of God', 'The Haystack in the Floods' and, to a lesser extent, 'Golden Wings'. The 'atmospheric' group consists of 'The Wind', 'The Blue Closet' and 'The Tune of Seven Towers'. Finally, 'Praise of My Lady' is a love poem in rhyming triplets in which the poet speaks for once in the first person; it expresses the quasi-mystical adoration (emphasized in the Latin refrain meaning 'My blessed Lady') of the young man for the wonderful woman with whom he had fallen in love, but the medievalizing manner provides distance and control.

The Defence of Guenevere

But, knowing now that they would have her speak,
She threw her wet hair backward from her brow,
Her hand close to her mouth touching her cheek,

As though she had had there a shameful blow,
And feeling it shameful to feel aught but shame
All through her heart, yet felt her cheek burned so,

She must a little touch it; like one lame
She walked away from Gauwaine, with her head
Still lifted up; and on her cheek of flame

The tears dried quick; she stopped at last and said:
"O knights and lords, it seems but little skill
To talk of well-known things past now and dead.

"God wot I ought to say, I have done ill,
And pray you all forgiveness heartily!
Because you must be right, such great lords – still

"Listen, suppose your time were come to die,
And you were quite alone and very weak;
Yea, laid a dying while very mightily

"The wind was ruffling up the narrow streak
Of river through your broad lands running well:
Suppose a hush should come, then some one speak:

"'One of these cloths is heaven, and one is hell,
Now choose one cloth for ever; which they be,
I will not tell you, you must somehow tell

"'Of your own strength and mightiness; here, see!'
Yea, yea, my lord, and you to ope your eyes,
At foot of your familiar bed to see

"A great God's angel standing, with such dyes,
Not known on earth, on his great wings, and hands
Held out two ways, light from the inner skies

"Showing him well, and making his commands
Seem to be God's commands, moreover, too,
Holding within his hands the cloths on wands;

"And one of these strange choosing cloths was blue,
Wavy and long, and one cut short and red;
No man could tell the better of the two.

"After a shivering half-hour you said:
'God help! heaven's colour, the blue;' and he said: 'hell.'
Perhaps you then would roll upon your bed,

"And cry to all good men that loved you well,
'Ah Christ! if only I had known, known, known;'
Launcelot went away, then I could tell,

"Like wisest man how all things would be, moan,
And roll and hurt myself, and long to die,
And yet fear much to die for what was sown.

"Nevertheless you, O Sir Gauwaine, lie,
Whatever may have happened through these years,
God knows I speak truth, saying that you lie."

Her voice was low at first, being full of tears,
But as it cleared, it grew full loud and shrill,
Growing a windy shriek in all men's ears,

A ringing in their startled brains, until
She said that Gauwaine lied, then her voice sunk,
And her great eyes began again to fill,

Though still she stood right up, and never shrunk,
But spoke on bravely, glorious lady fair!
Whatever tears her full lips may have drunk,

She stood, and seemed to think, and wrung her hair,
Spoke out at last with no more trace of shame,
With passionate twisting of her body there:

"It chanced upon a day that Launcelot came
To dwell at Arthur's court: at Christmas-time
This happened; when the heralds sung his name,

"'Son of King Ban of Benwick,' seemed to chime
Along with all the bells that rang that day,
O'er the white roofs, with little change of rhyme.

"Christmas and whitened winter passed away,
And over me the April sunshine came,
Made very awful with black hail-clouds, yea

"And in the Summer I grew white with flame,
And bowed my head down – Autumn, and the sick
Sure knowledge things would never be the same,

"However often Spring might be most thick
Of blossoms and buds, smote on me, and I grew
Careless of most things, let the clock tick, tick,

"To my unhappy pulse, that beat right through
My eager body; while I laughed out loud,
And let my lips curl up at false or true,

"Seemed cold and shallow without any cloud.
Behold my judges, then the cloths were brought;
While I was dizzied thus, old thoughts would crowd,

"Belonging to the time ere I was bought
By Arthur's great name and his little love;
Must I give up for ever then, I thought,

"That which I deemed would ever round me move
Glorifying all things; for a little word,
Scarce ever meant at all, must I now prove

"Stone-cold for ever? Pray you, does the Lord
Will that all folks should be quite happy and good?
I love God now a little, if this cord

"Were broken, once for all what striving could
Make me love anything in earth or heaven?
So day by day it grew, as if one should

"Slip slowly down some path worn smooth and even,
Down to a cool sea on a summer day;
Yet still in slipping there was some small leaven

"Of stretched hands catching small stones by the way,
Until one surely reached the sea at last,
And felt strange new joy as the worn head lay

"Back, with the hair like sea-weed; yea all past
Sweat of the forehead, dryness of the lips,
Washed utterly out by the dear waves o'ercast,

"In the lone sea, far off from any ships!
Do I not know now of a day in Spring?
No minute of that wild day ever slips

"From out my memory; I hear thrushes sing,
And wheresoever I may be, straightway
Thoughts of it all come up with most fresh sting:

"I was half mad with beauty on that day,
And went without my ladies all alone,
In a quiet garden walled round every way;

"I was right joyful of that wall of stone,
That shut the flowers and trees up with the sky,
And trebled all the beauty: to the bone,

"Yea right through to my heart, grown very shy
With weary thoughts, it pierced, and made me glad;
Exceedingly glad, and I knew verily,

"A little thing just then had made me mad;
I dared not think, as I was wont to do,
Sometimes, upon my beauty; if I had

"Held out my long hand up against the blue,
And, looking on the tenderly darken'd fingers,
Thought that by rights one ought to see quite through,

"There, see you, where the soft still light yet lingers,
Round by the edges; what should I have done,
If this had joined with yellow spotted singers,

"And startling green drawn upward by the sun?
But shouting, loosed out, see now! all my hair,
And trancedly stood watching the west wind run

"With faintest half-heard breathing sound – why there
I lose my head e'en now in doing this;
But shortly listen – In that garden fair

"Came Launcelot walking; this is true, the kiss
Wherewith we kissed in meeting that spring day,
I scarce dare talk of the remember'd bliss,

"When both our mouths went wandering in one way,
And aching sorely, met among the leaves;
Our hands being left behind strained far away.

"Never within a yard of my bright sleeves
Had Launcelot come before – and now, so nigh!
After that day why is it Guenevere grieves?

"Nevertheless you, O Sir Gauwaine, lie,
Whatever happened on through all those years,
God knows I speak truth, saying that you lie.

"Being such a lady could I weep these tears
If this were true? A great queen such as I
Having sinn'd this way, straight her conscience sears;

"And afterwards she liveth hatefully,
Slaying and poisoning, certes never weeps, –
Gauwaine, be friends now, speak me lovingly.

"Do I not see how God's dear pity creeps
All through your frame, and trembles in your mouth?
Remember in what grave your mother sleeps,

"Buried in some place far down in the south,
Men are forgetting as I speak to you;
By her head sever'd in that awful drouth

"Of pity that drew Agravaine's fell blow,
I pray your pity! let me not scream out
For ever after, when the shrill winds blow

"Through half your castle-locks! let me not shout
For ever after in the winter night
When you ride out alone! in battle-rout

"Let not my rusting tears make your sword light!
Ah! God of mercy, how he turns away!
So, ever must I dress me to the fight;

"So – let God's justice work! Gauwaine, I say,
See me hew down your proofs: yea, all men know
Even as you said how Mellyagraunce one day,

"One bitter day in *la Fausse Garde*, for so
All good knights held it after, saw –
Yea, sirs, by cursed unknightly outrage; though

"You, Gauwaine, held his word without a flaw,
This Mellyagraunce saw blood upon my bed –
Whose blood then pray you? is there any law

"To make a queen say why some spots of red
Lie on her coverlet? or will you say:
'Your hands are white, lady, as when you wed,

"'Where did you bleed?' and must I stammer out: 'Nay,
I blush indeed, fair lord, only to rend
My sleeve up to my shoulder, where there lay

"'A knife-point last night:' so must I defend
The honour of the lady Guenevere?
Not so, fair lords, even if the world should end

"This very day, and you were judges here
Instead of God. Did you see Mellyagraunce
When Launcelot stood by him? what white fear

"Curdled his blood, and how his teeth did dance,
His side sink in? as my knight cried and said:
'Slayer of unarm'd men, here is a chance!

"'Setter of traps, I pray you guard your head,
By God I am so glad to fight with you,
Stripper of ladies, that my hand feels lead

"'For driving weight; hurrah now! draw and do,
For all my wounds are moving in my breast,
And I am getting mad with waiting so.'

"He struck his hands together o'er the beast,
Who fell down flat and grovell'd at his feet,
And groan'd at being slain so young – 'at least.'

"My knight said: 'Rise you, sir, who are so fleet
At catching ladies, half-arm'd will I fight,
My left side all uncovered!' then I weet,

"Up sprang Sir Mellyagraunce with great delight
Upon his knave's face; not until just then
Did I quite hate him, as I saw my knight

"Along the lists look to my stake and pen
With such a joyous smile, it made me sigh
From agony beneath my waist-chain, when

"The fight began, and to me they drew nigh;
Ever Sir Launcelot kept him on the right,
And traversed warily, and ever high

"And fast leapt caitiff's sword, until my knight
Sudden threw up his sword to his left hand,
Caught it, and swung it; that was all the fight,

"Except a spout of blood on the hot land;
For it was hottest summer; and I know
I wonder'd how the fire, while I should stand,

"And burn, against the heat, would quiver so,
Yards above my head; thus these matters went;
Which things were only warnings of the woe

"That fell on me. Yet Mellyagraunce was shent,
For Mellyagraunce had fought against the Lord;
Therefore, my lords, take heed lest you be blent

"With all this wickedness; say no rash word
Against me, being so beautiful; my eyes,
Wept all away to grey, may bring some sword

"To drown you in your blood; see my breast rise,
Like waves of purple sea, as here I stand;
And how my arms are moved in wonderful wise,

"Yea also at my full heart's strong command,
See through my long throat how the words go up
In ripples to my mouth; how in my hand

"The shadow lies like wine within a cup
Of marvellously colour'd gold; yea now
This little wind is rising, look you up,

"And wonder how the light is falling so
Within my moving tresses: will you dare,
When you have looked a little on my brow,

"To say this thing is vile? or will you care
For any plausible lies of cunning woof,
When you can see my face with no lie there

"For ever? am I not a gracious proof –
'But in your chamber Launcelot was found' –
Is there a good knight then would stand aloof,

"When a queen says with gentle queenly sound:
'O true as steel, come now and talk with me,
I love to see your step upon the ground

" 'Unwavering, also well I love to see
That gracious smile light up your face, and hear
Your wonderful words, that all mean verily

" 'The thing they seem to mean: good friend, so dear
To me in everything, come here to-night,
Or else the hours will pass most dull and drear;

" 'If you come not, I fear this time I might
Get thinking over much of times gone by,
When I was young, and green hope was in sight:

" 'For no man cares now to know why I sigh;
And no man comes to sing me pleasant songs,
Nor any brings me the sweet flowers that lie

" 'So thick in the gardens; therefore one so longs
To see you, Launcelot; that we may be
Like children once again, free from all wrongs

" 'Just for one night.' Did he not come to me?
What thing could keep true Launcelot away
If I said, 'Come?' There was one less than three

"In my quiet room that night, and we were gay;
Till sudden I rose up, weak, pale, and sick,
Because a bawling broke our dream up, yea

"I looked at Launcelot's face and could not speak,
For he looked helpless too, for a little while;
Then I remember how I tried to shriek,

"And could not, but fell down; from tile to tile
The stones they threw up rattled o'er my head
And made me dizzier; till within a while

"My maids were all about me, and my head
On Launcelot's breast was being soothed away
From its white chattering, until Launcelot said –

"By God! I will not tell you more to-day,
Judge any way you will – what matters it?
You know quite well the story of that fray,

"How Launcelot still'd their bawling, the mad fit
That caught up Gauwaine – all, all, verily,
But just that which would save me; these things flit.

"Nevertheless you, O Sir Gauwaine, lie,
Whatever may have happen'd these long years,
God knows I speak truth, saying that you lie!

"All I have said is truth, by Christ's dear tears."
She would not speak another word, but stood
Turn'd sideways; listening, like a man who hears

His brother's trumpet sounding through the wood
Of his foes' lances. She lean'd eagerly,
And gave a slight spring sometimes, as she could

At last hear something really; joyfully
Her cheek grew crimson, as the headlong speed
Of the roan charger drew all men to see,
The knight who came was Launcelot at good need.

King Arthur's Tomb

Hot August noon – already on that day
   Since sunrise through the Wiltshire downs, most sad
Of mouth and eye, he had gone leagues of way;
   Ay and by night, till whether good or bad

He was, he knew not, though he knew perchance
   That he was Launcelot, the bravest knight
Of all who since the world was, have borne lance,
   Or swung their swords in wrong cause or in right.

Nay, he knew nothing now, except that where
   The Glastonbury gilded towers shine,
A lady dwelt, whose name was Guenevere;
   This he knew also; that some fingers twine,

Not only in a man's hair, even his heart,
    (Making him good or bad I mean,) but in his life,
Skies, earth, men's looks and deeds, all that has part,
    Not being ourselves, in that half-sleep, half-strife,

(Strange sleep, strange strife,) that men call living; so
    Was Launcelot most glad when the moon rose,
Because it brought new memories of her – "Lo,
    Between the trees a large moon, the wind lows

"Not loud, but as a cow begins to low,
    Wishing for strength to make the herdsman hear:
The ripe corn gathereth dew; yea, long ago,
    In the old garden life, my Guenevere

"Loved to sit still among the flowers, till night
    Had quite come on, hair loosen'd, for she said,
Smiling like heaven, that its fairness might
    Draw up the wind sooner to cool her head.

"Now while I ride how quick the moon gets small,
    As it did then – I tell myself a tale
That will not last beyond the whitewashed wall,
    Thoughts of some joust must help me through the vale,

"Keep this till after – How Sir Gareth ran
    A good course that day under my Queen's eyes,
And how she sway'd laughing at Dinadan –
    No – back again, the other thoughts will rise,

"And yet I think so fast 'twill end right soon –
    Verily then I think, that Guenevere,
Made sad by dew and wind and tree-barred moon,
    Did love me more than ever, was more dear

"To me than ever, she would let me lie
    And kiss her feet, or, if I sat behind,

Would drop her hand and arm most tenderly,
    And touch my mouth. And she would let me wind

"Her hair around my neck, so that it fell
    Upon my red robe, strange in the twilight
With many unnamed colours, till the bell
    Of her mouth on my cheek sent a delight

"Through all my ways of being; like the stroke
    Wherewith God threw all men upon the face
When he took Enoch, and when Enoch woke
    With a changed body in the happy place.

"Once, I remember, as I sat beside,
    She turn'd a little and laid back her head,
And slept upon my breast; I almost died
    In those night-watches with my love and dread.

"There lily-like she bow'd her head and slept,
    And I breathed low and did not dare to move,
But sat and quiver'd inwardly, thoughts crept,
    And frighten'd me with pulses of my Love.

"The stars shone out above the doubtful green
    Of her bodice, in the green sky overhead;
Pale in the green sky were the stars I ween,
    Because the moon shone like a star she shed

"When she dwelt up in heaven a while ago,
    And ruled all things but God: the night went on,
The wind grew cold, and the white moon grew low,
    One hand had fallen down, and now lay on

"My cold stiff palm; there were no colours then
    For near an hour, and I fell asleep
In spite of all my striving, even when
    I held her whose name-letters make me leap.

34

"I did not sleep long, feeling that in sleep
    I did some loved one wrong, so that the sun
Had only just arisen from the deep
    Still land of colours, when before me one

"Stood whom I knew, but scarcely dared to touch,
    She seemed to have changed so in the night;
Moreover she held scarlet lilies, such
    As Maiden Margaret bears upon the light

"Of the great church walls, natheless did I walk
    Through the fresh wet woods and the wheat that morn,
Touching her hair and hand and mouth, and talk
    Of love we held, nigh hid among the corn.

"Back to the palace, ere the sun grew high,
    We went, and in a cool green room all day
I gazed upon the arras giddily,
    Where the wind set the silken kings a-sway.

"I could not hold her hand, or see her face;
    For which may God forgive me! but I think,
Howsoever, that she was not in that place."
    These memories Launcelot was quick to drink;

And when these fell, some paces past the wall,
    There rose yet others, but they wearied more,
And tasted not so sweet; they did not fall
    So soon, but vaguely wrenched his strained heart sore

In shadowy slipping from his grasp: these gone,
    A longing followed; if he might but touch
That Guenevere at once! Still night, the lone
    Grey horse's head before him vex'd him much,

In steady nodding over the grey road –
    Still night, and night, and night, and emptied heart

35

Of any stories; what a dismal load
    Time grew at last, yea, when the night did part,

And let the sun flame over all, still there
    The horse's grey ears turn'd this way and that,
And still he watch'd them twitching in the glare
    Of the morning sun, behind them still he sat,

Quite wearied out with all the wretched night,
    Until about the dustiest of the day,
On the last down's brow he drew his rein in sight
    Of the Glastonbury roofs that choke the way.

And he was now quite giddy as before,
    When she slept by him, tired out, and her hair
Was mingled with the rushes on the floor,
    And he, being tired too, was scarce aware

Of her presence; yet as he sat and gazed,
    A shiver ran throughout him, and his breath
Came slower, he seem'd suddenly amazed,
    As though he had not heard of Arthur's death.

This for a moment only, presently
    He rode on giddy still, until he reach'd
A place of apple-trees, by the thorn-tree
    Wherefrom St. Joseph in the days past preached.

Dazed there he laid his head upon a tomb
    Not knowing it was Arthur's, at which sight
One of her maidens told her, "He is come,"
    And she went forth to meet him; yet a blight

Had settled on her, all her robes were black,
    With a long white veil only; she went slow,
As one walks to be slain, her eyes did lack
    Half her old glory, yea, alas! the glow

Had left her face and hands; this was because
  As she lay last night on her purple bed,
Wishing for morning, grudging every pause
  Of the palace clocks, until that Launcelot's head

Should lie on her breast, with all her golden hair
  Each side – when suddenly the thing grew drear
In morning twilight, when the grey downs bare
  Grew into lumps of sin to Guenevere.

At first she said no word, but lay quite still,
  Only her mouth was open, and her eyes
Gazed wretchedly about from hill to hill;
  As though she asked, not with so much surprise

As tired disgust, what made them stand up there
  So cold and grey. After, a spasm took
Her face, and all her frame; she caught her hair,
  All her hair, in both hands, terribly she shook,

And rose till she was sitting in the bed,
  Set her teeth hard, and shut her eyes and seem'd
As though she would have torn it from her head,
  Natheless she dropp'd it, lay down, as she deem'd

It matter'd not whatever she might do –
  O Lord Christ! pity on her ghastly face!
Those dismal hours while the cloudless blue
  Drew the sun higher – He did give her grace;

Because at last she rose up from her bed,
  And put her raiment on, and knelt before
The blessed rood, and with her dry lips said,
  Muttering the words against the marble floor:

"Unless you pardon, what shall I do, Lord,
  But go to hell? and there see day by day

Foul deed on deed, hear foulest word on word,
  For ever and ever, such as on the way

"To Camelot I heard once from a churl,
  That curled me up upon my jennet's neck
With bitter shame; how then, Lord, should I curl
  For ages and for ages? dost thou reck

"That I am beautiful, Lord, even as you
  And your dear Mother? why did I forget
You were so beautiful, and good, and true,
  That you loved me so, Guenevere? O yet

"If even I go to hell, I cannot choose
  But love you, Christ, yea, though I cannot keep
From loving Launcelot; O Christ! must I lose
  My own heart's love? see, though I cannot weep,

"Yet am I very sorry for my sin;
  Moreover, Christ, I cannot bear that hell,
I am most fain to love you, and to win
  A place in heaven some time – I cannot tell –

"Speak to me, Christ! I kiss, kiss, kiss your feet;
  Ah! now I weep!" – The maid said: "By the tomb
He waiteth for you, lady," coming fleet,
  Not knowing what woe filled up all the room.

So Guenevere rose and went to meet him there;
  He did not hear her coming, as he lay
On Arthur's head, till some of her long hair
  Brush'd on the new-cut stone – "Well done! to pray

"For Arthur, my dear lord, the greatest king
  That ever lived." "Guenevere! Guenevere!
Do you not know me, are you gone mad? fling
  Your arms and hair about me, lest I fear

"You are not Guenevere, but some other thing."
  "Pray you forgive me, fair lord Launcelot!
I am not mad, but I am sick; they cling,
  God's curses, unto such as I am; not

"Ever again shall we twine arms and lips."
  "Yea, she is mad: thy heavy law, O Lord,
Is very tight about her now, and grips
  Her poor heart, so that no right word

"Can reach her mouth; so, Lord, forgive her now,
  That she not knowing what she does, being mad,
Kills me in this way – Guenevere, bend low
  And kiss me once! for God's love kiss me! sad

"Though your face is, you look much kinder now;
  Yea once, once for the last time kiss me, lest I die."
"Christ! my hot lips are very near his brow,
  Help me to save his soul! – Yea, verily,

"Across my husband's head, fair Launcelot!
  Fair serpent mark'd with V upon the head!
This thing we did while yet he was alive,
  Why not, O twisting knight, now he is dead?

"Yea, shake! shake now and shiver! if you can
  Remember anything for agony,
Pray you remember how when the wind ran
  One cool spring evening through fair aspen-tree,

"And elm and oak about the palace there,
  The king came back from battle, and I stood
To meet him, with my ladies, on the stair,
  My face made beautiful with my young blood."

"Will she lie now, Lord God?" "Remember too,
  Wrung heart, how first before the knights there came

A royal bier, hung round with green and blue,
   Above it shone great tapers with sick flame.

"And thereupon Lucius, the Emperor,
   Lay royal-robed, but stone-cold now and dead,
Not able to hold sword or sceptre more,
   But not quite grim; because his cloven head

"Bore no marks now of Launcelot's bitter sword,
   Being by embalmers deftly solder'd up;
So still it seem'd the face of a great lord,
   Being mended as a craftsman mends a cup.

"Also the heralds sung rejoicingly
   To their long trumpets: 'Fallen under shield,
Here lieth Lucius, King of Italy,
   Slain by Lord Launcelot in open field.'

"Thereat the people shouted: 'Launcelot!'
   And through the spears I saw you drawing nigh,
You and Lord Arthur – nay, I saw you not,
   But rather Arthur, God would not let die,

"I hoped, these many years; he should grow great,
   And in his great arms still encircle me,
Kissing my face, half blinded with the heat
   Of king's love for the queen I used to be.

"Launcelot, Launcelot, why did he take your hand,
   When he had kissed me in his kingly way?
Saying: 'This is the knight whom all the land
   Calls Arthur's banner, sword and shield to-day;

"'Cherish him, love.' Why did your long lips cleave
   In such strange way unto my fingers then?
So eagerly glad to kiss, so loath to leave
   When you rose up? Why among helmed men

"Could I always tell you by your long strong arms,
    And sway like an angel's in your saddle there?
Why sicken'd I so often with alarms
    Over the tilt-yard? Why were you more fair

"Than aspens in the autumn at their best?
    Why did you fill all lands with your great fame,
So that Breuse even, as he rode, fear'd lest
    At turning of the way your shield should flame?

"Was it nought then, my agony and strife?
    When as day passed by day, year after year,
I found I could not live a righteous life!
    Didst ever think queens held their truth for dear?

"O, but your lips say: 'Yea, but she was cold
    Sometimes, always uncertain as the spring;
When I was sad she would be overbold,
    Longing for kisses;' when war-bells did ring,

"The back-toll'd bells of noisy Camelot –"
    "Now, Lord God, listen! listen, Guenevere,
Though I am weak just now, I think there's not
    A man who dares to say: 'You hated her,

"'And left her moaning while you fought your fill
    In the daisied meadows!' lo you her thin hand,
That on the carven stone can not keep still,
    Because she loves me against God's command,

"Has often been quite wet with tear on tear,
    Tears Launcelot keeps somewhere, surely not
In his own heart, perhaps in Heaven, where
    He will not be these ages" – "Launcelot!

"Loud lips, wrung heart! I say when the bells rang,
    The noisy back-toll'd bells of Camelot,

41

There were two spots on earth, the thrushes sang
   In the lonely gardens where my love was not,

"Where I was almost weeping; I dared not
   Weep quite in those days, lest one maid should say,
In tittering whispers: 'Where is Launcelot
   To wipe with some kerchief those tears away?'

"Another answer sharply with brows knit,
   And warning hand up, scarcely lower though:
'You speak too loud, see you, she heareth it,
   This tigress fair has claws, as I well know,

"'As Launcelot knows too, the poor knight! well-a-day!
   Why met he not with Iseult from the West,
Or better still, Iseult of Brittany,
   Perchance indeed quite ladyless were best.'

"Alas, my maids, you loved not overmuch
   Queen Guenevere, uncertain as sunshine
In March; forgive me! for my sin in being such,
   About my whole life, all my deeds did twine,

"Made me quite wicked; as I found out then,
   I think; in the lonely palace where each morn
We went, my maids and I, to say prayers when
   They sang mass in the chapel on the lawn.

"And every morn I scarce could pray at all,
   For Launcelot's red-golden hair would play,
Instead of sunlight, on the painted wall,
   Mingled with dreams of what the priest did say;

"Grim curses out of Peter and of Paul;
   Judging of strange sins in Leviticus;
Another sort of writing on the wall,
   Scored deep across the painted heads of us.

"Christ sitting with the woman at the well,
    And Mary Magdalen repenting there,
Her dimmed eyes scorch'd and red at sight of hell
    So hardly 'scaped, no gold light on her hair.

"And if the priest said anything that seemed
    To touch upon the sin they said we did, –
(This in their teeth) they looked as if they deem'd
    That I was spying what thoughts might be hid

"Under green-cover'd bosoms, heaving quick
    Beneath quick thoughts; while they grew red with shame,
And gazed down at their feet – while I felt sick,
    And almost shriek'd if one should call my name.

"The thrushes sang in the lone garden there –
    But where you were the birds were scared I trow –
Clanging of arms about pavilions fair,
    Mixed with the knights' laughs; there, as I well know,

"Rode Launcelot, the king of all the band,
    And scowling Gauwaine, like the night in day,
And handsome Gareth, with his great white hand
    Curl'd round the helm-crest, ere he join'd the fray;

"And merry Dinadan with sharp dark face,
    All true knights loved to see; and in the fight
Great Tristram, and though helmed you could trace
    In all his bearing the frank noble knight;

"And by him Palomydes; helmet off,
    He fought, his face brush'd by his hair,
Red heavy swinging hair; he fear'd a scoff
    So overmuch, though what true knight would dare

"To mock that face, fretted with useless care,
    And bitter useless striving after love?

43

O Palomydes, with much honour bear
  Beast Glatysaunt upon your shield, above

"Your helm that hides the swinging of your hair,
  And think of Iseult, as your sword drives through
Much mail and plate – O God, let me be there
  A little time, as I was long ago!

"Because stout Gareth lets his spear fall low,
  Gauwaine and Launcelot and Dinadan
Are helm'd and waiting; let the trumpets go!
  Bend over, ladies, to see all you can!

"Clench teeth, dames, yea, clasp hands, for Gareth's spear
  Throws Kay from out his saddle, like a stone
From a castle-window when the foe draws near –
  'Iseult!' Sir Dinadan rolleth overthrown.

"'Iseult!' – again – the pieces of each spear
  Fly fathoms up, and both the great steeds reel;
'Tristram for Iseult!' 'Iseult!' and 'Guenevere!'
  The ladies' names bite verily like steel.

"They bite – bite me, Lord God! – I shall go mad,
  Or else die kissing him, he is so pale;
He thinks me mad already, O bad! bad!
  Let me lie down a little while and wail."

"No longer so, rise up, I pray you, love,
  And slay me really, then we shall be heal'd,
Perchance, in the aftertime by God above."
  "Banner of Arthur – with black-bended shield

"Sinister-wise across the fair gold ground!
  Here let me tell you what a knight you are,
O sword and shield of Arthur! you are found
  A crooked sword, I think, that leaves a scar

44

"On the bearer's arm, so be he thinks it straight,
    Twisted Malay's crease beautiful blue-grey,
Poison'd with sweet fruit; as he found too late,
    My husband Arthur, on some bitter day!

"O sickle cutting hemlock the day long!
    That the husbandman across his shoulder hangs,
And, going homeward about evensong,
    Dies the next morning, struck through by the fangs!

"Banner and sword and shield, you dare not pray to die,
    Lest you meet Arthur in the other world,
And knowing who you are, he pass you by,
    Taking short turns that he may watch you curl'd,

"Body and face and limbs in agony,
    Lest he weep presently and go away,
Saying: 'I loved him once,' with a sad sigh –
    Now I have slain him, Lord, let me go too, I pray.
                                    Launcelot *falls*.

"Alas! alas! I know not what to do,
    If I run fast it is perchance that I
May fall and stun myself, much better so,
    Never, never again! not even when I die."

Launcelot *on awaking*.

I stretch'd my hands towards her and fell down,
    How long I lay in swoon I cannot tell:
My head and hands were bleeding from the stone.
    When I rose up, also I heard a bell.

Near Avalon

A ship with shields before the sun,
Six maidens round the mast,
A red-gold crown on every one,
A green gown on the last.

The fluttering green banners there
Are wrought with ladies' heads most fair,
And a portraiture of Guenevere
The middle of each sail doth bear.

A ship with sails before the wind,
And round the helm six knights,
Their heaumes are on, whereby, half blind,
They pass by many sights.

The tatter'd scarlet banners there
Right soon will leave the spear-heads bare.
Those six knights sorrowfully bear
In all their heaumes some yellow hair.

The Haystack in the Floods

Had she come all the way for this,
To part at last without a kiss?
Yea, had she borne the dirt and rain
That her own eyes might see him slain
Beside the haystack in the floods?

Along the dripping leafless woods,
The stirrup touching either shoe,
She rode astride as troopers do;
With kirtle kilted to her knee,

To which the mud splash'd wretchedly;
And the wet dripp'd from every tree
Upon her head and heavy hair,
And on her eyelids broad and fair;
The tears and rain ran down her face.
By fits and starts they rode apace,
And very often was his place
Far off from her; he had to ride
Ahead, to see what might betide
When the roads cross'd; and sometimes, when
There rose a murmuring from his men,
Had to turn back with promises;
Ah me! she had but little ease;
And often for pure doubt and dread
She sobb'd, made giddy in the head
By the swift riding; while, for cold,
Her slender fingers scarce could hold
The wet reins; yea, and scarcely, too,
She felt the foot within her shoe
Against the stirrup: all for this,
To part at last without a kiss
Beside the haystack in the floods.

For when they near'd that old soak'd hay,
They saw across the only way
That Judas, Godmar, and the three
Red running lions dismally
Grinn'd from his pennon, under which
In one straight line along the ditch,
They counted thirty heads.

So then,
While Robert turn'd round to his men,
She saw at once the wretched end,
And, stooping down, tried hard to rend
Her coif the wrong way from her head,
And hid her eyes; while Robert said:

"Nay, love, 'tis scarcely two to one,
At Poictiers where we made them run
So fast – why, sweet my love, good cheer,
The Gascon frontier is so near,
Nought after this."

                 But, "O!" she said,
"My God! my God! I have to tread
The long way back without you; then
The court at Paris; those six men;
The gratings of the Chatelet;
The swift Seine on some rainy day
Like this, and people standing by
And laughing, while my weak hands try
To recollect how strong men swim.
All this, or else a life with him,
For which I should be damned at last.
Would God that this next hour were past!"

He answer'd not, but cried his cry,
"St. George for Marny!" cheerily;
And laid his hand upon her rein.
Alas! no man of all his train
Gave back that cheery cry again:
And, while for rage his thumb beat fast
Upon his sword-hilts, some one cast
About his neck a kerchief long,
And bound him.

             Then they went along
To Godmar; who said: "Now, Jehane,
Your lover's life is on the wane
So fast, that, if this very hour
You yield not as my paramour,
He will not see the rain leave off –
Nay, keep your tongue from gibe and scoff,
Sir Robert, or I slay you now."

She laid her hand upon her brow,
Then gazed upon the palm, as though
She thought her forehead bled, and – "No!"
She said, and turn'd her head away,
As there were nothing else to say,
And everything were settled: red
Grew Godmar's face from chin to head:
"Jehane, on yonder hill there stands
My castle, guarding well my lands:
What hinders me from taking you,
And doing that I list to do
To your fair wilful body, while
Your knight lies dead?"

                  A wicked smile
Wrinkled her face, her lips grew thin,
A long way out she thrust her chin:
"You know that I should strangle you
While you were sleeping; or bite through
Your throat, by God's help – ah!" she said,
"Lord Jesus, pity your poor maid!
For in such wise they hem me in,
I cannot choose but sin and sin,
Whatever happens: yet I think
They could not make me eat or drink,
And so should I just reach my rest."
"Nay, if you do not my behest,
O Jehane! though I love you well,"
Said Godmar, "would I fail to tell
All that I know?" "Foul lies," she said.
"Eh? lies, my Jehane? by God's head,
At Paris folks would deem them true!
Do you know, Jehane, they cry for you:
'Jehane the brown! Jehane the brown!
Give us Jehane to burn or drown!' –
Eh – gag me Robert! – sweet my friend,
This were indeed a piteous end

For those long fingers, and long feet,
And long neck, and smooth shoulders sweet;
An end that few men would forget
That saw it. So, an hour yet:
Consider, Jehane, which to take
Of life or death!"

       So, scarce awake,
Dismounting, did she leave that place,
And totter some yards: with her face
Turn'd upward to the sky she lay,
Her head on a wet heap of hay,
And fell asleep: and while she slept,
And did not dream, the minutes crept
Round to the twelve again; but she,
Being waked at last, sigh'd quietly,
And strangely childlike came, and said:
"I will not." Straightway Godmar's head,
As though it hung on strong wires, turn'd
Most sharply round, and his face burn'd.

For Robert – both his eyes were dry,
He could not weep, but gloomily
He seem'd to watch the rain; yea, too,
His lips were firm; he tried once more
To touch her lips; she reach'd out, sore
And vain desire so tortured them,
The poor grey lips, and now the hem
Of his sleeve brush'd them.

       With a start
Up Godmar rose, thrust them apart;
From Robert's throat he loosed the bands
Of silk and mail; with empty hands
Held out, she stood and gazed, and saw
The long bright blade without a flaw
Glide out from Godmar's sheath, his hand

In Robert's hair; she saw him bend
Back Robert's head; she saw him send
The thin steel down; the blow told well,
Right backward the knight Robert fell,
And moaned as dogs do, being half dead,
Unwitting, as I deem: so then
Godmar turn'd grinning to his men,
Who ran, some five or six, and beat
His head to pieces at their feet.

Then Godmar turn'd again and said:
"So, Jehane, the first fitte is read!
Take note, my lady, that your way
Lies backward to the Chatelet!"
She shook her head and gazed awhile
At her cold hands with a rueful smile,
As though this thing had made her mad.

This was the parting that they had
Beside the haystack in the floods.

Concerning Geffray Teste Noire

And if you meet the Canon of Chimay,
  As going to Ortaise you well may do,
Greet him from John of Castel Neuf, and say,
  All that I tell you, for all this is true.

This Geffray Teste Noire was a Gascon thief,
  Who, under shadow of the English name,
Pilled all such towns and countries as were lief
  To King Charles and St. Denis; thought it blame

If anything escaped him; so my lord
   The Duke of Berry sent Sir John Bonne Lance,
And other knights, good players with the sword,
   To check this thief and give the land a chance.

Therefore we set our bastides round the tower
   That Geffray held, the strong thief! like a king,
High perch'd upon the rock of Ventadour,
   Hopelessly strong by Christ! It was mid spring,

When first I joined the little army there
   With ten good spears; Auvergne is hot, each day
We sweated armed before the barrier;
   Good feats of arms were done there often – eh?

Your brother was slain there? I mind me now,
   A right good man-at-arms, God pardon him!
I think 'twas Geffray smote him on the brow
   With some spiked axe, and while he totter'd, dim

About the eyes, the spear of Alleyne Roux
   Slipped through his camaille and his throat; well, well!
Alleyne is paid now; your name Alleyne too?
   Mary! how strange – but this tale I would tell –

For spite of all our bastides, damned Blackhead
   Would ride abroad whene'er he chose to ride,
We could not stop him; many a burgher bled
   Dear gold all round his girdle; far and wide

The villaynes dwelt in utter misery
   'Twixt us and thief Sir Geffray; hauled this way
By Sir Bonne Lance at one time, he gone by,
   Down comes this Teste Noire on another day,

And therefore they dig up the stone, grind corn,
   Hew wood, draw water, yea, they lived, in short,

As I said just now, utterly forlorn,
    Till this our knave and Blackhead was out-fought.

So Bonne Lance fretted, thinking of some trap
    Day after day, till on a time he said:
"John of Newcastle, if we have good hap,
    We catch our thief in two days." "How?" I said.

"Why, Sir, to-day he rideth out again,
    Hoping to take well certain sumpter mules
From Carcassonne, going with little train,
    Because, forsooth, he thinketh us mere fools;

"But if we set an ambush in some wood,
    He is but dead: so, Sir, take thirty spears
To Verville forest, if it seem you good."
    Then felt I like the horse in Job, who hears

The dancing trumpet sound, and we went forth;
    And my red lion on the spear-head flapped,
As faster than the cool wind we rode north,
    Towards the wood of Verville; thus it happed.

We rode a soft pace on that day, while spies
    Got news about Sir Geffray; the red wine
Under the road-side bush was clear; the flies,
    The dragon-flies I mind me most, did shine

In brighter arms than ever I put on;
    So – "Geffray," said our spies, "would pass that way
Next day at sundown:" then he must be won;
    And so we enter'd Verville wood next day,

In the afternoon; through it the highway runs,
    'Twixt copses of green hazel, very thick,
And underneath, with glimmering of suns,
    The primroses are happy; the dews lick

53

The soft green moss. "Put cloths about your arms,
  Lest they should glitter; surely they will go
In a long thin line, watchful for alarms,
  With all their carriages of booty; so –

"Lay down my pennon in the grass – Lord God!
  What have we lying here? will they be cold,
I wonder, being so bare, above the sod,
  Instead of under? This was a knight too, fold

"Lying on fold of ancient rusted mail;
  No plate at all, gold rowels to the spurs,
And see the quiet gleam of turquoise pale
  Along the ceinture; but the long time blurs

"Even the tinder of his coat to nought,
  Except these scraps of leather; see how white
The skull is, loose within the coif! He fought
  A good fight, maybe, ere he was slain quite.

"No armour on the legs too; strange in faith –
  A little skeleton for a knight, though – ah!
This one is bigger, truly without scathe
  His enemies escaped not – ribs driven out far –

"That must have reach'd the heart, I doubt – how now,
  What say you, Aldovrand – a woman? why?"
"Under the coif a gold wreath on the brow,
  Yea, see the hair not gone to powder, lie,

"Golden, no doubt, once – yea, and very small
  This for a knight; but for a dame, my lord,
These loose-hung bones seem shapely still, and tall, –
  Didst ever see a woman's bones, my lord?"

Often, God help me! I remember when
  I was a simple boy, fifteen years old,

The Jacquerie froze up the blood of men
  With their fell deeds, not fit now to be told:

God help again! we enter'd Beauvais town,
  Slaying them fast, whereto I help'd, mere boy
As I was then; we gentles cut them down,
  These burners and defilers, with great joy.

Reason for that, too: in the great church there
  These fiends had lit a fire, that soon went out,
The church at Beauvais being so great and fair –
  My father, who was by me, gave a shout

Between a beast's howl and a woman's scream,
  Then, panting, chuckled to me: "John, look! look!
Count the dames' skeletons!" from some bad dream
  Like a man just awaked, my father shook;

And I, being faint with smelling the burnt bones,
  And very hot with fighting down the street,
And sick of such a life, fell down, with groans
  My head went weakly nodding to my feet.

– An arrow had gone through her tender throat,
  And her right wrist was broken; then I saw
The reason why she had on that war-coat,
  Their story came out clear without a flaw;

For when he knew that they were being waylaid,
  He threw it over her, yea, hood and all;
Whereby he was much hack'd, while they were stay'd
  By those their murderers; many an one did fall

Beneath his arm, no doubt, so that he clear'd
  Their circle, bore his death-wound out of it;
But as they rode, some archer least afear'd
  Drew a strong bow, and thereby she was hit.

Still as he rode he knew not she was dead,
  Thought her but fainted from her broken wrist,
He bound with his great leathern belt – she bled?
  Who knows! he bled too, neither was there miss'd

The beating of her heart, his heart beat well
  For both of them, till here, within this wood,
He died scarce sorry; easy this to tell;
  After these years the flowers forget their blood. –

How could it be? never before that day,
  However much a soldier I might be,
Could I look on a skeleton and say
  I care not for it, shudder not – now see,

Over those bones I sat and pored for hours,
  And thought, and dream'd, and still I scarce could see
The small white bones that lay upon the flowers,
  But evermore I saw the lady; she

With her dear gentle walking leading in,
  By a chain of silver twined about her wrists,
Her loving knight, mounted and arm'd to win
  Great honour for her, fighting in the lists.

O most pale face, that brings such joy and sorrow
  Into men's hearts – yea, too, so piercing sharp
That joy is, that it marcheth nigh to sorrow
  For ever – like an overwinded harp. –

Your face must hurt me always; pray you now,
  Doth it not hurt you too? seemeth some pain
To hold you always, pain to hold your brow
  So smooth, unwrinkled ever; yea again,

Your long eyes where the lids seem like to drop,
  Would you not, lady, were they shut fast, feel

Far merrier? there so high they will not stop,
   They are most sly to glide forth and to steal

Into my heart; *I kiss their soft lids there,*
   And in green gardens scarce can stop my lips
From wandering on your face, but that your hair
   Falls down and tangles me, back my face slips.

Or say your mouth – I saw you drink red wine
   Once at a feast; how slowly it sank in,
As though you fear'd that some wild fate might twine
   Within that cup, and slay you for a sin.

And when you talk your lips do arch and move
   In such wise that a language new I know
Besides their sound; they quiver, too, with love
   When you are standing silent; know this, too,

I saw you kissing once, like a curved sword
   That bites with all its edge, did your lips lie,
Curled gently, slowly, long time could afford
   For caught-up breathings; like a dying sigh

They gather'd up their lines and went away,
   And still kept twitching with a sort of smile,
As likely to be weeping presently, –
   Your hands too – how I watch'd them all the while!

"Cry out St. Peter now," quoth Aldovrand;
   I cried, "St. Peter!" broke out from the wood
With all my spears; we met them hand to hand,
   And shortly slew them; natheless, by the rood,

We caught not Blackhead then, or any day;
   Months after that he died at last in bed,
From a wound pick'd up at a barrier-fray;
   That same year's end a steel bolt in the head,

And much bad living kill'd Teste Noire at last;
    John Froissart knoweth he is dead by now,
No doubt, but knoweth not this tale just past;
    Perchance then you can tell him what I show.

In my new castle, down beside the Eure,
    There is a little chapel of squared stone,
Painted inside and out; in green nook pure
    There did I lay them, every wearied bone;

And over it they lay, with stone-white hands
    Clasped fast together, hair made bright with gold;
This Jaques Picard, known throughout many lands,
    Wrought cunningly; he's dead now – I am old.

The Judgment of God

"Swerve to the left, son Roger," he said,
    "When you catch his eyes through the helmet-slit,
Swerve to the left, then out at his head,
    And the Lord God give you joy of it!"

The blue owls on my father's hood
    Were a little dimm'd as I turn'd away;
This giving up of blood for blood
    Will finish here somehow to-day.

So – when I walk'd out from the tent,
    Their howling almost blinded me;
Yet for all that I was not bent
    By any shame. Hard by, the sea

Made a noise like the aspens where
    We did that wrong, but now the place

Is very pleasant, and the air
　　Blows cool on any passer's face.

And all the wrong is gather'd now
　　Into the circle of these lists –
Yea, howl out, butchers! tell me how
　　His hands were cut off at the wrists;

And how Lord Roger bore his face
　　A league above his spear-point, high
Above the owls, to that strong place
　　Among the waters – yea, yea, cry:

"What a brave champion we have got!
　　Sir Oliver, the flower of all
The Hainault knights!" The day being hot,
　　He sat beneath a broad white pall,

White linen over all his steel;
　　What a good knight he look'd! his sword
Laid athwart his knees; he liked to feel
　　Its steadfast edge clear as his word.

And he look'd solemn; how his love
　　Smiled whitely on him, sick with fear!
How all the ladies up above
　　Twisted their pretty hands! so near

The fighting was – Ellayne! Ellayne!
　　They cannot love like you can, who
Would burn your hands off, if that pain
　　Could win a kiss – am I not true

To you for ever? therefore I
　　Do not fear death or anything;
If I should limp home wounded, why,
　　While I lay sick you would but sing,

And soothe me into quiet sleep.
   If they spat on the recreaunt knight,
Threw stones at him, and cursed him deep,
   Why then – what then; your hand would light

So gently on his drawn-up face,
   And you would kiss him, and in soft
Cool scented clothes would lap him, pace
   The quiet room and weep oft, – oft

Would turn and smile, and brush his cheek
   With your sweet chin and mouth; and in
The order'd garden you would seek
   The biggest roses – any sin.

And these say: "No more now my knight,
   Or God's knight any longer" – you,
Being than they so much more white,
   So much more pure and good and true,

Will cling to me for ever – there,
   Is not that wrong turn'd right at last
Through all these years, and I wash'd clean?
   Say, yea, Ellayne; the time is past,

Since on that Christmas-day last year
   Up to your feet the fire crept,
And the smoke through the brown leaves sere
   Blinded your dear eyes that you wept;

Was it not I that caught you then,
   And kiss'd you on the saddle-bow?
Did not the blue owl mark the men
   Whose spears stood like the corn a-row?

This Oliver is a right good knight,
   And must needs beat me, as I fear,

Unless I catch him in the fight,
　My father's crafty way – John, here!

Bring up the men from the south gate,
　To help me if I fall or win,
For even if I beat, their hate
　Will grow to more than this mere grin.

Golden Wings

Midways of a wallèd garden,
　In the happy poplar land,
　Did an ancient castle stand,
With an old knight for a warden.

Many scarlet bricks there were
　In its walls, and old grey stone;
　Over which red apples shone
At the right time of the year.

On the bricks the green moss grew,
　Yellow lichen on the stone,
　Over which red apples shone;
Little war that castle knew.

Deep green water fill'd the moat,
　Each side had a red-brick lip,
　Green and mossy with the drip
Of dew and rain; there was a boat

Of carven wood, with hangings green
　About the stern; it was great bliss
　For lovers to sit there and kiss
In the hot summer noons, not seen.

Across the moat the fresh west wind
   In very little ripples went;
   The way the heavy aspens bent
Towards it, was a thing to mind.

The painted drawbridge over it
   Went up and down with gilded chains.
   'Twas pleasant in the summer rains
Within the bridge-house there to sit.

There were five swans that ne'er did eat
   The water-weeds, for ladies came
   Each day, and young knights did the same,
And gave them cakes and bread for meat.

They had a house of painted wood,
   A red roof gold-spiked over it,
   Wherein upon their eggs to sit
Week after week; no drop of blood,

Drawn from men's bodies by sword-blows,
   Came ever there, or any tear;
   Most certainly from year to year
'Twas pleasant as a Provence rose.

The banners seem'd quite full of ease,
   That over the turret-roofs hung down;
   The battlements could get no frown
From the flower-moulded cornices.

Who walked in that garden there?
   Miles and Giles and Isabeau,
   Tall Jehane du Castel beau,
Alice of the golden hair,

Big Sir Gervaise, the good knight,
   Fair Ellayne le Violet,

Mary, Constance fille de fay,
Many dames with footfall light.

Whosoever wander'd there,
  Whether it be dame or knight,
  Half of scarlet, half of white
Their raiment was; of roses fair

Each wore a garland on the head,
  At Ladies' Gard the way was so:
  Fair Jehane du Castel beau
Wore her wreath till it was dead.

Little joy she had of it,
  Of the raiment white and red,
  Or the garland on her head,
She had none with whom to sit

In the carven boat at noon;
  None the more did Jehane weep,
  She would only stand and keep
Saying: "He will be here soon."

Many times in the long day
  Miles and Giles and Gervaise passed,
  Holding each some white hand fast,
Every time they heard her say:

"Summer cometh to an end,
  Undern cometh after noon;
  Golden wings will be here soon,
What if I some token send?"

Wherefore that night within the hall,
  With open mouth and open eyes,
  Like some one listening with surprise,
She sat before the sight of all.

63

Stoop'd down a little she sat there,
   With neck stretch'd out and chin thrown up,
   One hand around a golden cup;
And strangely with her fingers fair

She beat some tune upon the gold;
   The minstrels in the gallery
   Sung: "Arthur, who will never die,
In Avallon he groweth old."

And when the song was ended, she
   Rose and caught up her gown and ran;
   None stopp'd her eager face and wan
Of all that pleasant company.

Right so within her own chamber
   Upon her bed she sat; and drew
   Her breath in quick gasps; till she knew
That no man follow'd after her.

She took the garland from her head,
   Loosed all her hair, and let it lie
   Upon the coverlit; thereby
She laid the gown of white and red;

And she took off her scarlet shoon,
   And bared her feet; still more and more
   Her sweet face redden'd; evermore
She murmur'd: "He will be here soon;

"Truly he cannot fail to know
   My tender body waits him here;
   And if he knows, I have no fear
For poor Jehane du Castel beau."

She took a sword within her hand,
   Whose hilts were silver, and she sung

Somehow like this, wild words that rung
A long way over the moonlit land:

Gold wings across the sea!
Grey light from tree to tree,
Gold hair beside my knee,
I pray thee come to me,
Gold wings!

The water slips,
The red-bill'd moorhen dips.
Sweet kisses on red lips;
Alas! the red rust grips,
And the blood-red dagger rips,
Yet, O knight, come to me!

Are not my blue eyes sweet?
The west wind from the wheat
Blows cold across my feet;
Is it not time to meet
Gold wings across the sea?

White swans on the green moat,
Small feathers left afloat
By the blue-painted boat;
Swift running of the stoat;
Sweet gurgling note by note
Of sweet music.

O gold wings,
Listen how gold hair sings,
And the Ladies' Castle rings,
Gold wings across the sea.

I sit on a purple bed,
Outside, the wall is red,
Thereby the apple hangs,
And the wasp, caught by the fangs,

Dies in the autumn night,
And the bat flits till light,
And the love-crazèd knight

Kisses the long wet grass:
The weary days pass, –
Gold wings across the sea!

Gold wings across the sea!
Moonlight from tree to tree,
Sweet hair laid on my knee,
O, sweet knight, come to me!

Gold wings, the short night slips,
The white swan's long neck drips,
I pray thee, kiss my lips,
Gold wings across the sea.

No answer through the moonlit night;
    No answer in the cold grey dawn;
    No answer when the shaven lawn
Grew green, and all the roses bright.

Her tired feet look'd cold and thin,
    Her lips were twitch'd, and wretched tears,
    Some, as she lay, roll'd past her ears,
Some fell from off her quivering chin.

Her long throat, stretched to its full length,
    Rose up and fell right brokenly;
    As though the unhappy heart was nigh
Striving to break with all its strength.

And when she slipp'd from off the bed,
    Her cramp'd feet would not hold her; she
    Sank down and crept on hand and knee,
On the window-sill she laid her head.

There, with crookèd arm upon the sill,
   She look'd out, muttering dismally:
   "There is no sail upon the sea,
No pennon on the empty hill.

"I cannot stay here all alone,
   Or meet their happy faces here,
   And wretchedly I have no fear;
A little while, and I am gone."

Therewith she rose upon her feet,
   And totter'd; cold and misery
   Still made the deep sobs come, till she
At last stretch'd out her fingers sweet,

And caught the great sword in her hand;
   And, stealing down the silent stair,
   Barefooted in the morning air,
And only in her smock, did stand

Upright upon the green lawn grass;
   And hope grew in her as she said:
   "I have thrown off the white and red,
And pray God it may come to pass

"I meet him; if ten years go by
   Before I meet him; if, indeed,
   Meanwhile both soul and body bleed,
Yet there is end of misery,

"And I have hope. He could not come,
   But I can go to him and show
   These new things I have got to know,
And make him speak, who has been dumb."

O Jehane! the red morning sun
   Changed her white feet to glowing gold,

Upon her smock, on crease and fold,
Changed that to gold which had been dun.

O Miles and Giles and Isabeau,
 Fair Ellayne le Violet,
 Mary, Constance fille de fay!
Where is Jehane du Castel beau?

O big Gervaise, ride a-pace!
 Down to the hard yellow sand,
 Where the water meets the land.
This is Jehane by her face;

Why has she a broken sword?
 Mary! she is slain outright;
 Verily a piteous sight;
Take her up without a word!

Giles and Miles and Gervaise there,
 Ladies' Gard must meet the war;
 Whatsoever knights these are,
Man the walls withouten fear!

Axes to the apple-trees,
 Axes to the aspens tall!
 Barriers without the wall
May be lightly made of these.

O poor shivering Isabeau;
 Poor Ellayne le Violet,
 Bent with fear! we miss to-day
Brave Jehane du Castel beau.

O poor Mary, weeping so!
 Wretched Constance fille de fay!
 Verily we miss to-day
Fair Jehane du Castel beau.

The apples now grow green and sour
   Upon the mouldering castle-wall,
   Before they ripen there they fall:
There are no banners on the tower.

The draggled swans most eagerly eat
   The green weeds trailing in the moat;
   Inside the rotting leaky boat
You see a slain man's stiffen'd feet.

The Wind

Ah! no, no, it is nothing, surely nothing at all,
Only the wild-going wind round by the garden-wall,
For the dawn just now is breaking, the wind beginning to fall.

> *Wind, wind! thou art sad, art thou kind?*
> *Wind, wind, unhappy! thou art blind,*
> *Yet still thou wanderest the lily-seed to find.*

So I will sit, and think and think of the days gone by,
Never moving my chair for fear the dogs should cry,
Making no noise at all while the flambeau burns awry.

For my chair is heavy and carved, and with sweeping green behind
It is hung, and the dragons thereon grin out in the gusts of the
   wind;
On its folds an orange lies, with a deep gash cut in the rind.

> *Wind, wind! thou art sad, art thou kind?*
> *Wind, wind, unhappy! thou art blind,*
> *Yet still thou wanderest the lily-seed to find.*

If I move my chair it will scream, and the orange will roll out far,
And the faint yellow juice ooze out like blood from a wizard's jar;
And the dogs will howl for those who went last month to the war.

> *Wind, wind! thou art sad, art thou kind?*
> *Wind, wind, unhappy! thou art blind,*
> *Yet still thou wanderest the lily-seed to find.*

So I will sit and think of love that is over and past,
O! so long ago – yes, I will be quiet at last;
Whether I like it or not, a grim half-slumber is cast

Over my worn old brains, that touches the roots of my heart,
And above my half-shut eyes the blue roof 'gins to part,
And show the blue spring sky, till I am ready to start

From out of the green-hung chair; but something keeps me still,
And I fall in a dream that I walk'd with her on the side of a hill,
Dotted – for was it not spring? – with tufts of the daffodil.

> *Wind, wind! thou art sad, art thou kind?*
> *Wind, wind, unhappy! thou art blind,*
> *Yet still thou wanderest the lily-seed to find.*

And Margaret as she walk'd held a painted book in her hand;
Her finger kept the place; I caught her, we both did stand
Face to face, on the top of the highest hill in the land.

> *Wind, wind! thou art sad, art thou kind?*
> *Wind, wind, unhappy! thou art blind,*
> *Yet still thou wanderest the lily-seed to find.*

I held to her long bare arms, but she shudder'd away from me,
While the flush went out of her face as her head fell back on a tree,
And a spasm caught her mouth, fearful for me to see;

And still I held to her arms till her shoulder touch'd my mail,
Weeping she totter'd forward, so glad that I should prevail,
And her hair went over my robe, like a gold flag over a sail.

> *Wind, wind! thou art sad, art thou kind?*
> *Wind, wind, unhappy! thou art blind,*
> *Yet still thou wanderest the lily-seed to find.*

I kiss'd her hard by the ear, and she kiss'd me on the brow,
And then lay down on the grass, where the mark on the moss is
    now,
And spread her arms out wide while I went down below.

       Wind, wind! thou art sad, art thou kind?
       Wind, wind, unhappy! thou art blind,
       Yet still thou wanderest the lily-seed to find.

And then I walk'd for a space to and fro on the side of the hill,
Till I gather'd and held in my arms great sheaves of the daffodil,
And when I came again my Margaret lay there still.

I piled them high and high above her heaving breast,
How they were caught and held in her loose ungirded vest!
But one beneath her arm died, happy so to be prest!

       Wind, wind! thou art sad, art thou kind?
       Wind, wind, unhappy! thou art blind,
       Yet still thou wanderest the lily-seed to find.

Again I turn'd my back and went away for an hour;
She said no word when I came again, so, flower by flower,
I counted the daffodils over, and cast them languidly lower.

       Wind, wind! thou art sad, art thou kind?
       Wind, wind, unhappy! thou art blind,
       Yet still thou wanderest the lily-seed to find.

My dry hands shook & shook as the green gown show'd again,
Clear'd from the yellow flowers, and I grew hollow with pain,
And on to us both there fell from the sun-shower drops of rain.

       Wind, wind! thou art sad, art thou kind?
       Wind, wind, unhappy! thou art blind,
       Yet still thou wanderest the lily-seed to find.

Alas! alas! there was blood on the very quiet breast,
Blood lay in the many folds of the loose ungirded vest,
Blood lay upon her arm where the flower had been prest.

I shriek'd and leapt from my chair, and the orange roll'd out far,
The faint yellow juice oozed out like blood from a wizard's jar;
And then in march'd the ghosts of those that had gone to the war.

I knew them by the arms that I was used to paint
Upon their long thin shields; but the colours were all grown faint,
And faint upon their banner was Olaf, king and saint.

> *Wind, wind! thou art sad, art thou kind?*
> *Wind, wind, unhappy! thou art blind,*
> *Yet still thou wanderest the lily-seed to find.*

The Blue Closet

THE DAMOZELS
Lady Alice, Lady Louise,
Between the wash of the tumbling seas
We are ready to sing, if so ye please;
So lay your long hands on the keys;
         Sing: *"Laudate pueri."*

And ever the great bell overhead
Boom'd in the wind a knell for the dead,
Though no one toll'd it, a knell for the dead.

LADY LOUISE
Sister, let the measure swell
Not too loud; for you sing not well
If you drown the faint boom of the bell;
         He is weary, so am I.

And ever the chevron overhead
Flapp'd on the banner of the dead;
(Was he asleep, or was he dead?)

LADY ALICE
Alice the Queen, and Louise the Queen,
Two damozels wearing purple and green,
Four lone ladies dwelling here
From day to day and year to year;
And there is none to let us go;
To break the locks of the doors below,
Or shovel away the heaped-up snow;
And when we die no man will know
That we are dead; but they give us leave,
Once every year on Christmas-eve,
To sing in the Closet Blue one song;
And we should be so long, so long,
If we dared, in singing; for dream on dream,
They float on in a happy stream;
Float from the gold strings, float from the keys,
Float from the open'd lips of Louise;
But, alas! the sea-salt oozes through
The chinks of the tiles of the Closet Blue;
And ever the great bell overhead
Booms in the wind a knell for the dead,
The wind plays on it a knell for the dead.

They sing all together.

How long ago was it, how long ago,
He came to this tower with hands full of snow?

"Kneel down, O love Louise, kneel down!" he said,
And sprinkled the dusty snow over my head.

He watch'd the snow melting, it ran through my hair,
Ran over my shoulders, white shoulders and bare.

73

"I cannot weep for thee, poor love Louise,
For my tears are all hidden deep under the seas;

"In a gold and blue casket she keeps all my tears,
But my eyes are no longer blue, as in old years;

"Yea, they grow grey with time, grow small and dry,
I am so feeble now, would I might die."

And in truth the great bell overhead
Left off his pealing for the dead,
Perchance, because the wind was dead.

Will he come back again, or is he dead?
O! is he sleeping, my scarf round his head?

Or did they strangle him as he lay there,
With the long scarlet scarf I used to wear?

Only I pray thee, Lord, let him come here!
Both his soul and his body to me are most dear.

Dear Lord, that loves me, I wait to receive
Either body or spirit this wild Christmas-eve.

Through the floor shot up a lily red,
With a patch of earth from the land of the dead,
For he was strong in the land of the dead.

What matter that his cheeks were pale,
  His kind kiss'd lips all grey?
"O, love Louise, have you waited long?"
  "O, my lord Arthur, yea."

What if his hair that brush'd her cheek
  Was stiff with frozen rime?
His eyes were grown quite blue again,
  As in the happy time.

74

"O, love Louise, this is the key
    Of the happy golden land!
O, sisters, cross the bridge with me,
    My eyes are full of sand.
What matter that I cannot see,
    If ye take me by the hand?"

And ever the great bell overhead,
And the tumbling seas mourn'd for the dead;
For their song ceased, and they were dead.

The Tune of Seven Towers

No one goes there now:
    For what is left to fetch away
From the desolate battlements all arow,
    And the lead roof heavy and grey?
"Therefore," said fair Yoland of the flowers,
"This is the tune of Seven Towers."

No one walks there now;
    Except in the white moonlight
The white ghosts walk in a row;
    If one could see it, an awful sight, –
"Listen!" said fair Yoland of the flowers,
"This is the tune of Seven Towers."

But none can see them now,
    Though they sit by the side of the moat,
Feet half in the water, there in a row,
    Long hair in the wind afloat.
"Therefore," said fair Yoland of the flowers,
"This is the tune of Seven Towers."

If any will go to it now,
    He must go to it all alone,
  Its gates will not open to any row
    Of glittering spears – will *you* go alone?
"Listen!" said fair Yoland of the flowers,
"This is the tune of Seven Towers."

  By my love go there now,
    To fetch me my coif away,
  My coif and my kirtle, with pearls arow,
    Oliver, go to-day!
"Therefore," said fair Yoland of the flowers,
"This is the tune of Seven Towers."

  I am unhappy now,
    I cannot tell you why;
  If you go, the priests and I in a row
    Will pray that you may not die.
"Listen!" said fair Yoland of the flowers,
"This is the tune of Seven Towers."

  If you will go for me now,
    I will kiss your mouth at last;
        [*She sayeth inwardly*]
    (*The graves stand grey in a row.*)
    Oliver, hold me fast!
"Therefore," said fair Yoland of the flowers,
"This is the tune of Seven Towers."

Praise of My Lady

My lady seems of ivory
Forehead, straight nose, and cheeks that be
Hollow'd a little mournfully.
    Beata mea Domina!

Her forehead, overshadow'd much
By bows of hair, has a wave such
As God was good to make for me.
    Beata mea Domina!

Not greatly long my lady's hair,
Nor yet with yellow colour fair,
But thick and crispèd wonderfully:
    Beata mea Domina!

Heavy to make the pale face sad,
And dark, but dead as though it had
Been forged by God most wonderfully
   – *Beata mea Domina!* –

Of some strange metal, thread by thread,
To stand out from my lady's head,
Not moving much to tangle me.
    Beata mea Domina!

Beneath her brows the lids fall slow,
The lashes a clear shadow throw
Where I would wish my lips to be.
    Beata mea Domina!

Her great eyes, standing far apart,
Draw up some memory from her heart,
And gaze out very mournfully;
   – *Beata mea Domina!* –

So beautiful and kind they are,
But most times looking out afar,
Waiting for something, not for me.
                    Beata mea Domina!

I wonder if the lashes long
Are those that do her bright eyes wrong,
For always half tears seem to be
            – Beata mea Domina! –

Lurking below the underlid,
Darkening the place where they lie hid –
If they should rise and flow for me!
                    Beata mea Domina!

Her full lips being made to kiss,
Curl'd up and pensive each one is;
This makes me faint to stand and see.
                    Beata mea Domina!

Her lips are not contented now,
Because the hours pass so slow
Towards a sweet time: (pray for me,)
            – Beata mea Domina! –

Nay, hold thy peace! for who can tell?
But this at least I know full well,
Her lips are parted longingly,
                – Beata mea Domina! –

So passionate and swift to move,
To pluck at any flying love,
That I grow faint to stand and see.
                    Beata mea Domina!

Yea! there beneath them is her chin,
So fine and round, it were a sin
To feel no weaker when I see
                – Beata mea Domina! –

God's dealings; for with so much care
And troublous, faint lines wrought in there,
He finishes her face for me.
                    Beata mea Domina!

Of her long neck what shall I say?
What things about her body's sway,
Like a knight's pennon or slim tree
                    – *Beata mea Domina!* –

Set gently waving in the wind;
Or her long hands that I may find
On some day sweet to move o'er me?
                    Beata mea Domina!

God pity me though, if I miss'd
The telling, how along her wrist
The veins creep, dying languidly
                    – *Beata mea Domina!* –

Inside her tender palm and thin.
Now give me pardon, dear, wherein
My voice is weak and vexes thee.
                    Beata mea Domina!

All men that see her any time,
I charge you straightly in this rhyme,
What, and wherever you may be,
                    – *Beata mea Domina!* –

To kneel before her; as for me,
I choke and grow quite faint to see
My lady moving graciously.
                    Beata mea Domina!

THE LIFE AND DEATH OF JASON
1867

This long narrative poem established Morris's popularity with the reading public. Morris incorporated into the blank-verse narrative a number of lyrical poems, four of which are included here. The first, from Book IV, is sung by the sea-nymph who lures Hylas into her realm: it tells of love lost and still sought. The second, from Book X, is sung to the Argonauts by the bard Orpheus: it speaks movingly of 'Saturn's days of gold', the legendary golden age, and calls on Lyaeus to lead the mariners and give purpose to their lives. The third, from Book XII, is also sung by Orpheus, as they travel on swiftly towards their goal: it looks forward to a successful outcome of the journey. The fourth, from Book XIV, is sung by the Hesperides, keepers of the Golden Apples, as the mariners regretfully leave the garden to go on their way: it tells of how the garden alone retains the beauty of the vanished golden age.

(i)

"I know a little garden-close
Set thick with lily and red rose,
Where I would wander if I might
From dewy dawn to dewy night,
And have one with me wandering.

"And though within it no birds sing,
And though no pillared house is there,
And though the apple boughs are bare
Of fruit and blossom, would to God,
Her feet upon the green grass trod,
And I beheld them as before.

"There comes a murmur from the shore,
And in the place two fair streams are,
Drawn from the purple hills afar,
Drawn down unto the restless sea;
The hills whose flowers ne'er fed the bee,
The shore no ship has ever seen,
Still beaten by the billows green,

Whose murmur comes unceasingly
Unto the place for which I cry.
   "For which I cry both day and night,
For which I let slip all delight,
That maketh me both deaf and blind,
Careless to win, unskilled to find,
And quick to lose what all men seek.
   "Yet tottering as I am and weak,
Still have I left a little breath
To seek within the jaws of death
An entrance to that happy place,
To seek the unforgotten face
Once seen, once kissed, once reft from me
Anigh the murmuring of the sea."

(ii)

   "Alas! for Saturn's days of gold,
Before the mountain men were bold
To dig up iron from the earth
Wherewith to slaughter health and mirth,
And bury hope far underground.
When all things needful did abound
In every land; nor must men toil,
Nor wear their lives in strife to foil
Each other's hands, for all was good,
And no man knew the sight of blood.
   "With all the world man had no strife,
No element against his life
Was sworn and bitter; on the sea,
Dry-shod, could all walk easily;
No fire there was but what made day,
Or hidden in the mountains grey;
No pestilence, no lightning flash,
No over-mastering wind, to dash
The roof upon some trembling head.

"Then the year changed, but ne'er was dead,
Nor was the autumn-tide more sad
Than very spring; and all unclad
Folk went upon the harmless snow,
For not yet did mid-winter know
The biting frost and icy wind,
The very east was soft and kind.

"And on the crown of July days,
All heedless of the mid-day blaze,
Unshaded by the rosy bowers,
Unscorched beside the tulip flowers,
The snow-white naked girl might stand;
Or fearless thrust her tender hand
Amidst the thornless rose bushes.

"Then, 'mid the twilight of the trees
None feared the yellow beast to meet;
Smiling to feel their languid feet
Licked by the serpent's forkèd tongue.
For then no clattering horn had rung
Through those green glades, or made afraid
The timid dwellers in the shade.
No lust of strength, no fear of death
Had driven men, with shortened breath,
The stag's wide-open eyes to watch;
No shafts to slay, no nets to catch,
Were yet; unyoked the neat might play
On untilled meads and mountains grey;
Unshorn the silly sheep might rove.

"Nor knew that world consuming love,
Mother of hate, or envy cold,
Or rage for fame, or thirst for gold,
Or longing for the ways untried,
Which ravening and unsatisfied,
Draw shortened lives of men to hell.

"Alas! what profit now to tell
The long unweary lives of men

Of past days – threescore years and ten,
Unbent, unwrinkled, beautiful,
Regarding not death's flower-crowned skull,
But with some damsel intertwined
In such love as leaves hope behind.
  "Alas, the vanished days of bliss!
Will no God send some dream of this,
That we may know what it has been?

  "O thou, the chapleted with green,
Thou purple-stained, but not with blood,
Who on the edge of some cool wood
Forgettest the grim Indian plain,
And all the strife and all the pain,
While in thy sight the must foams out,
And maid and man, with cry and shout,
Toil while thou laughest, think of us,
And drive away these piteous
Formless and wailing thoughts, that press
About our hour of happiness.
  "Lyæus, King! by thee alone
To song may change our tuneless moan,
The murmur of the bitter sea
To ancient tales be changed by thee.
By thee the unnamed smouldering fire
Within our hearts turns to desire
Sweet, amorous, half-satisfied;
Through thee the doubtful years untried
Seem fair to us and fortunate,
In spite of death, in spite of Fate."

"O death, that maketh life so sweet,
O fear, with mirth before thy feet,
What have ye yet in store for us,
The conquerors, the glorious?
    "Men say: 'For fear that thou shouldst die
To-morrow, let to-day pass by
Flower-crowned and singing;' yet have we
Passed our to-day upon the sea,
Or in a poisonous unknown land,
With fear and death on either hand,
And listless when the day was done
Have scarcely hoped to see the sun
Dawn on the morrow of the earth,
Nor in our hearts have thought of mirth.
And while the world lasts, scarce again
Shall any sons of men bear pain
Like we have borne, yet be alive.
    "So surely not in vain we strive
Like other men for our reward;
Sweet peace and deep, the chequered sward
Beneath the ancient mulberry-trees,
The smooth-paved gilded palaces,
Where the shy thin-clad damsels sweet
Make music with their gold-ringed feet.
The fountain court amidst of it,
Where the short-haired slave maidens sit,
While on the veinèd pavement lie
The honied things and spicery
Their arms have borne from out the town.
    "The dancers on the thymy down
In summer twilight, when the earth
Is still of all things but their mirth,
And echoes borne upon the wind
Of others in like way entwined:

"The merchant-town's fair market-place,
Where over many a changing face
The pigeons of the temple flit,
And still the outland merchants sit
Like kings above their merchandise,
Lying to foolish men and wise:

"Ah! if they heard that we were come
Into the bay, and bringing home
That which all men have talked about,
Some men with rage, and some with doubt,
Some with desire, and some with praise;
Then would the people throng the ways,
Nor heed the outland merchandise,
Nor any talk, from fools or wise,
But tales of our accomplished quest.

"What soul within the house shall rest
When we come home? The wily king
Shall leave his throne to see the thing;
No man shall keep the landward gate,
The hurried traveller shall wait
Until our bulwarks graze the quay;
Unslain the milk-white bull shall be
Beside the quivering altar-flame;
Scarce shall the maiden clasp for shame
Over her breast the raiment thin
The morn that Argo cometh in.

"Then cometh happy life again
That payeth well our toil and pain
In that sweet hour, when all our woe
But as a pensive tale we know,
Nor yet remember deadly fear;
For surely now if death be near,
Unthought-of is it, and unseen
When sweet is, that hath bitter been."

"O ye, who to this place have strayed,
That never for man's eyes was made,
Depart in haste, as ye have come,
And bear back to your sea-beat home
This memory of the age of gold,
And for your eyes, grown over-bold,
Your hearts shall pay in sorrowing,
For want of many a half-seen thing.

"Lo, such as is this garden green,
In days past, all the world has been,
And what we know all people knew,
Save this, that unto worse all grew.
    "But since the golden age is gone,
This little place is left alone,
Unchanged, unchanging, watched of us,
The daughters of wise Hesperus.
    "Surely the heavenly Messenger
Full oft is fain to enter here,
And yet without must he abide;
Nor longeth less the dark king's bride
To set red lips unto that fruit
That erst made nought her mother's suit.
Here would Diana rest awhile,
Forgetful of her woodland guile,
Among these beasts that fear her nought.
Nor is it less in Pallas' thought,
Beneath our trees to ponder o'er
The wide, unfathomed sea of lore;
And oft-kissed Citheræa, no less
Weary of love, full fain would press
These flowers with soft unsandalled feet.

"But unto us our rest is sweet,
Neither shall any man or God

Or lovely Goddess touch the sod
Where-under old times buried lie,
Before the world knew misery.
Nor will we have a slave or king,
Nor yet will we learn anything
But that we know, that makes us glad;
While oft the very Gods are sad
With knowing what the Fates shall do.
   "Neither from us shall wisdom go
To fill the hungering hearts of men,
Lest to them threescore years and ten
Come but to seem a little day,
Once given, and taken soon away.
Nay, rather let them find their life
Bitter and sweet, fulfilled of strife,
Restless with hope, vain with regret,
Trembling with fear, most strangely set
'Twixt memory and forgetfulness;
So more shall joy be, troubles less,
And surely when all this is past,
They shall not want their rest at last.

   "Let earth and heaven go on their way,
While still we watch from day to day,
In this green place left all alone,
A remnant of the days long gone."

THE EARTHLY PARADISE
1868-1870

This long poem or collection of poems confirmed Morris's reputation with the reading public. It appeared in three volumes: Volume I (containing parts 1 and 2) in May 1868, Volume II (part 3) in December 1869 (dated 1870), and Volume III (part 4) in December 1870. The twenty-four narrative poems that constitute the main body of the work are too lengthy for inclusion here. The collection is represented by the framing poems, an introductory 'Apology' and a concluding 'Envoi'; the fine poems for each of the twelve months; and two particularly beautiful songs from the stories (comparable to those in *Jason*): 'Oh dwellers on this lovely Earth', sung by Apollo as a herdsman in Thessaly in the June story, 'The Love of Alcestis', and 'In the white-flowered hawthorn brake', a song for two voices, female and male, overheard by the hero of the August poem, 'Ogier the Dane'.

Apology

Of Heaven or Hell I have no power to sing,
I cannot ease the burden of your fears,
Or make quick-coming death a little thing,
Or bring again the pleasure of past years,
Nor for my words shall ye forget your tears,
Or hope again for aught that I can say,
The idle singer of an empty day.

But rather, when aweary of your mirth,
From full hearts still unsatisfied ye sigh,
And, feeling kindly unto all the earth,
Grudge every minute as it passes by,
Made the more mindful that the sweet days die –
Remember me a little then I pray,
The idle singer of an empty day.

The heavy trouble, the bewildering care
That weighs us down who live and earn our bread,
These idle verses have no power to bear;
So let me sing of names rememberèd,
Because they, living not, can ne'er be dead,
Or long time take their memory quite away
From us poor singers of an empty day.

Dreamer of dreams, born out of my due time,
Why should I strive to set the crooked straight?
Let it suffice me that my murmuring rhyme
Beats with light wing against the ivory gate,
Telling a tale not too importunate
To those who in the sleepy region stay,
Lulled by the singer of an empty day.

Folk say, a wizard to a northern king
At Christmas-tide such wondrous things did show,
That through one window men beheld the spring,
And through another saw the summer glow,
And through a third the fruited vines a-row,
While still, unheard, but in its wonted way,
Piped the drear wind of that December day.

So with this Earthly Paradise it is,
If ye will read aright, and pardon me,
Who strive to build a shadowy isle of bliss
Midmost the beating of the steely sea,
Where tossed about all hearts of men must be;
Whose ravening monsters mighty men shall slay,
Not the poor singer of an empty day.

March

Slayer of the winter, art thou here again?
O welcome, thou that bring'st the summer nigh!
The bitter wind makes not thy victory vain,
Nor will we mock thee for thy faint blue sky.
Welcome, O March! whose kindly days and dry
Make April ready for the throstle's song,
Thou first redresser of the winter's wrong!

Yea, welcome March! and though I die ere June,
Yet for the hope of life I give thee praise,
Striving to swell the burden of the tune
That even now I hear thy brown birds raise,
Unmindful of the past or coming days;
Who sing: "O joy! a new year is begun:
What happiness to look upon the sun!"

Ah, what begetteth all this storm of bliss
But Death himself, who crying solemnly,
E'en from the heart of sweet Forgetfulness,
Bids us "Rejoice, lest pleasureless ye die.
Within a little time must ye go by.
Stretch forth your open hands, and while ye live
Take all the gifts that Death and Life may give."

April

O fair midspring, besung so oft and oft,
How can I praise thy loveliness enow?
Thy sun that burns not, and thy breezes soft
That o'er the blossoms of the orchard blow,
The thousand things that 'neath the young leaves grow,
The hopes and chances of the growing year,
Winter forgotten long, and summer near.

When Summer brings the lily and the rose,
She brings us fear; her very death she brings
Hid in her anxious heart, the forge of woes;
And, dull with fear, no more the mavis sings.
But thou! thou diest not, but thy fresh life clings
About the fainting autumn's sweet decay,
When in the earth the hopeful seed they lay.

Ah! life of all the year, why yet do I
Amid thy snowy blossoms' fragrant drift,
Still long for that which never draweth nigh,
Striving my pleasure from my pain to sift,
Some weight from off my fluttering mirth to lift?
Now, when far bells are ringing, "Come again,
Come back, past years! why will ye pass in vain?"

May

O love, this morn when the sweet nightingale
Had so long finished all he had to say,
That thou hadst slept, and sleep had told his tale;
And midst a peaceful dream had stolen away
In fragrant dawning of the first of May,
Didst thou see aught? didst thou hear voices sing
Ere to the risen sun the bells 'gan ring?

For then methought the Lord of Love went by
To take possession of his flowery throne,
Ringed round with maids, and youths, and minstrelsy;
A little while I sighed to find him gone,
A little while the dawning was alone,
And the light gathered; then I held my breath,
And shuddered at the sight of Eld and Death.

Alas! Love passed me in the twilight dun,
His music hushed the wakening ousel's song;
But on these twain shone out the golden sun,
And o'er their heads the brown bird's tune was strong,
As shivering, 'twixt the trees they stole along;
None noted aught their noiseless passing by,
The world had quite forgotten it must die.

June

O June, O June, that we desired so,
Wilt thou not make us happy on this day?
Across the river thy soft breezes blow
Sweet with the scent of beanfields far away,
Above our heads rustle the aspens grey,
Calm is the sky with harmless clouds beset,
No thought of storm the morning vexes yet.

See, we have left our hopes and fears behind
To give our very hearts up unto thee;
What better place than this then could we find
By this sweet stream that knows not of the sea,
That guesses not the city's misery,
This little stream whose hamlets scarce have names,
This far-off, lonely mother of the Thames?

Here then, O June, thy kindness will we take;
And if indeed but pensive men we seem,
What should we do? thou wouldst not have us wake
From out the arms of this rare happy dream
And wish to leave the murmur of the stream,
The rustling boughs, the twitter of the birds,
And all thy thousand peaceful happy words.

July

Fair was the morn to-day, the blossom's scent
Floated across the fresh grass, and the bees
With low vexed song from rose to lily went,
A gentle wind was in the heavy trees,
And thine eyes shone with joyous memories;
Fair was the early morn and fair wert thou,
And I was happy – Ah, be happy now!

Peace and content without us, love within
That hour there was, now thunder and wild rain
Have wrapped the cowering world, and foolish sin
And nameless pride have made us wise in vain;
Ah, love! although the morn shall come again,
And on new rose-buds the new sun shall smile,
Can we regain what we have lost meanwhile?

E'en now the west grows clear of storm and threat,
But midst the lightning did the fair sun die –
Ah, he shall rise again for ages yet,
He cannot waste his life; but thou and I?
Who knows if next morn this felicity
My lips may feel, or if thou still shalt live
This seal of love renewed once more to give?

August

Across the gap made by our English hinds,
Amidst the Roman's handiwork, behold
Far off the long-roofed church; the shepherd binds
The withy round the hurdles of his fold
Down in the foss the river fed of old,
That through long lapse of time has grown to be
The little grassy valley that you see.

Rest here awhile, not yet the eve is still,
The bees are wandering yet, and you may hear
The barley mowers on the trenchèd hill,
The sheep-bells, and the restless changing weir,
All little sounds made musical and clear
Beneath the sky that burning August gives,
While yet the thought of glorious Summer lives.

Ah, love! such happy days, such days as these,
Must we still waste them, craving for the best,
Like lovers o'er the painted images
Of those who once their yearning hearts have blessed?
Have we been happy on our day of rest?
Thine eyes say "yes," but if it came again,
Perchance its ending would not seem so vain.

September

O come at last, to whom the springtide's hope
Looked for through blossoms, what hast thou for me?
Green grows the grass upon the dewy slope
Beneath thy gold-hung, grey-leaved apple-tree
Moveless, e'en as the autumn fain would be
That shades its sad eyes from the rising sun
And weeps at eve because the day is done.

What vision wilt thou give me, autumn morn,
To make thy pensive sweetness more complete?
What tale, ne'er to be told, of folk unborn?
What images of grey-clad damsels sweet
Shall cross thy sward with dainty noiseless feet?
What nameless shamefast longings made alive,
Soft-eyed September, will thy sad heart give?

Look long, O longing eyes, and look in vain!
Strain idly, aching heart, and yet be wise,
And hope no more for things to come again
That thou beheldest once with careless eyes!
Like a new-wakened man thou art, who tries
To dream again the dream that made him glad
When in his arms his loving love he had.

October

O love, turn from the unchanging sea, and gaze
Down these grey slopes upon the year grown old,
A-dying mid the autumn-scented haze,
That hangeth o'er the hollow in the wold,
Where the wind-bitten ancient elms enfold
Grey church, long barn, orchard, and red-roofed stead,
Wrought in dead days for men a long while dead.

Come down, O love; may not our hands still meet,
Since still we live to-day, forgetting June,
Forgetting May, deeming October sweet –
– O hearken, hearken! through the afternoon,
The grey tower sings a strange old tinkling tune!
Sweet, sweet, and sad, the toiling year's last breath,
Too satiate of life to strive with death.

And we too – will it not be soft and kind,
That rest from life, from patience and from pain,
That rest from bliss we know not when we find,
That rest from Love which ne'er the end can gain? –
– Hark, how the tune swells, that erewhile did wane!
Look up, love! – ah, cling close and never move!
How can I have enough of life and love?

November

Are thine eyes weary? is thy heart too sick
To struggle any more with doubt and thought,
Whose formless veil draws darkening now and thick
Across thee, e'en as smoke-tinged mist-wreaths brought
Down a fair dale to make it blind and nought?
Art thou so weary that no world there seems
Beyond these four walls, hung with pain and dreams?

Look out upon the real world, where the moon,
Half-way 'twixt root and crown of these high trees,
Turns the dread midnight into dreamy noon,
Silent and full of wonders, for the breeze
Died at the sunset, and no images,
No hopes of day, are left in sky or earth –
Is it not fair, and of most wondrous worth?

Yea, I have looked and seen November there;
The changeless seal of change it seemed to be,
Fair death of things that, living once, were fair;
Bright sign of loneliness too great for me,
Strange image of the dread eternity,
In whose void patience how can these have part,
These outstretched feverish hands, this restless heart?

December

Dead lonely night and all streets quiet now,
Thin o'er the moon the hindmost cloud swims past
Of that great rack that brought us up the snow;
On earth strange shadows o'er the snow are cast;
Pale stars, bright moon, swift cloud make heaven so vast
That earth left silent by the wind of night
Seems shrunken 'neath the grey unmeasured height.

Ah! through the hush the looked-for midnight clangs!
And then, e'en while its last stroke's solemn drone
In the cold air by unlit windows hangs,
Out break the bells above the year foredone,
Change, kindness lost, love left unloved alone;
Till their despairing sweetness makes thee deem
Thou once wert loved, if but amidst a dream.

O thou who clingest still to life and love,
Though nought of good, no God thou mayst discern,
Though nought that is, thine utmost woe can move,
Though no soul knows wherewith thine heart doth yearn,
Yet, since thy weary lips no curse can learn,
Cast no least thing thou lovedst once away,
Since yet perchance thine eyes shall see the day.

January

From this dull rainy undersky and low,
This murky ending of a leaden day,
That never knew the sun, this half-thawed snow,
These tossing black boughs faint against the grey
Of gathering night, thou turnest, dear, away
Silent, but with thy scarce-seen kindly smile
Sent though the dusk my longing to beguile.

There, the lights gleam, and all is dark without!
And in the sudden change our eyes meet dazed –
O look, love, look again! the veil of doubt
Just for one flash, past counting, then was raised!
O eyes of heaven, as clear thy sweet soul blazed
On mine a moment! O come back again,
Strange rest and dear amid the long dull pain!

Nay, nay, gone by! though there she sitteth still,
With wide grey eyes so frank and fathomless –
Be patient, heart, thy days they yet shall fill
With utter rest – Yea, now thy pain they bless,
And feed thy last hope of the world's redress –
O unseen hurrying rack! O wailing wind!
What rest and where go ye this night to find?

February

Noon – and the north-west sweeps the empty road,
The rain-washed fields from hedge to hedge are bare;
Beneath the leafless elms some hind's abode
Looks small and void, and no smoke meets the air
From its poor hearth: one lonely rook doth dare
The gale, and beats above the unseen corn,
Then turns, and whirling down the wind is borne.

Shall it not hap that on some dawn of May
Thou shalt awake, and, thinking of days dead,
See nothing clear but this same dreary day,
Of all the days that have passed o'er thine head?
Shalt thou not wonder, looking from thy bed,
Through green leaves on the windless east a-fire,
That this day too thine heart doth still desire?

Shalt thou not wonder that it liveth yet,
The useless hope, the useless craving pain,
That made thy face, that lonely noontide, wet
With more than beating of the chilly rain?
Shalt thou not hope for joy new born again,
Since no grief ever born can ever die
Through changeless change of seasons passing by?

Song from 'The Love of Alcestis'

O dwellers on the lovely earth,
Why will ye break your rest and mirth
To weary us with fruitless prayer;
Why will ye toil and take such care
For children's children yet unborn,
And garner store of strife and scorn
To gain a scarce-remembered name,
Cumbered with lies and soiled with shame?
And if the gods care not for you,
What is this folly ye must do
To win some mortal's feeble heart?
O fools! when each man plays his part,
And heeds his fellow little more
Than these blue waves that kiss the shore
Take heed of how the daisies grow.
O fools! and if ye could but know
How fair a world to you is given.

O brooder on the hills of heaven,
When for my sin thou drav'st me forth,
Hadst thou forgot what this was worth,
Thine own hand had made? The tears of men,
The death of threescore years and ten,
The trembling of the timorous race –
Had these things so bedimmed the place
Thine own hand made, thou couldst not know
To what a heaven the earth might grow
If fear beneath the earth were laid,
If hope failed not, nor love decayed.

Song from 'Ogier the Dane'

HÆC

In the white-flowered hawthorn brake,
Love, be merry for my sake;
Twine the blossoms in my hair,
Kiss me where I am most fair –
Kiss me, love! for who knoweth
What thing cometh after death?

ILLE

Nay, the garlanded gold hair
Hides thee where thou art most fair;
Hides the rose-tinged hills of snow –
Ah, sweet love, I have thee now!
Kiss me, love! for who knoweth
What thing cometh after death?

HÆC

Shall we weep for a dead day,
Or set Sorrow in our way?
Hidden by my golden hair,
Wilt thou weep that sweet days wear?
Kiss me, love! for who knoweth
What thing cometh after death?

ILLE

Weep, O Love, the days that flit,
  Now, while I can feel thy breath;
Then may I remember it
  Sad and old, and near my death.
Kiss me, love! for who knoweth
What thing cometh after death?

L'Envoi

Here are we for the last time face to face,
Thou and I, Book, before I bid thee speed
Upon thy perilous journey to that place
For which I have done on thee pilgrim's weed,
Striving to get thee all things for thy need –
– I love thee, whatso time or men may say
Of the poor singer of an empty day.

Good reason why I love thee, e'en if thou
Be mocked or clean forgot as time wears on;
For ever as thy fashioning did grow,
Kind word and praise because of thee I won
From those without whom were my world all gone,
My hope fallen dead, my singing cast away,
And I set soothly in an empty day.

I love thee; yet this last time must it be
That thou must hold thy peace and I must speak,
Lest if thou babble I begin to see
Thy gear too thin, thy limbs and heart too weak,
To find the land thou goest forth to seek –
– Though what harm if thou die upon the way,
Thou idle singer of an empty day?

But though this land desired thou never reach,
Yet folk who know it mayst thou meet or death,
Therefore a word unto thee would I teach
To answer these, who, noting thy weak breath,
Thy wandering eyes, thy heart of little faith,
May make thy fond desire a sport and play,
Mocking the singer of an empty day.

That land's name, say'st thou? and the road thereto?
Nay, Book, thou mockest, saying thou know'st it not;
Surely no book of verse I ever knew

101

But ever was the heart within him hot
To gain the Land of Matters Unforgot –
– There, now we both laugh – as the whole world may,
At us poor singers of an empty day.

Nay, let it pass, and hearken! Hast thou heard
That therein I believe I have a friend,
Of whom for love I may not be afeard?
It is to him indeed I bid thee wend;
Yea, he perchance may meet thee ere thou end,
Dying so far off from the hedge of bay,
Thou idle singer of an empty day!

Well, think of him, I bid thee, on the road,
And if it hap that midst of thy defeat,
Fainting beneath thy follies' heavy load,
My Master, GEOFFREY CHAUCER, thou do meet,
Then shalt thou win a space of rest full sweet;
Then be thou bold, and speak the words I say,
The idle singer of an empty day!

"O Master, O thou great of heart and tongue,
Thou well mayst ask me why I wander here,
In raiment rent of stories oft besung!
But of thy gentleness draw thou anear,
And then the heart of one who held thee dear
Mayst thou behold! So near as that I lay
Unto the singer of an empty day.

"For this he ever said, who sent me forth
To seek a place amid thy company;
That howsoever little was my worth,
Yet was he worth e'en just so much as I;
He said that rhyme hath little skill to lie;
Nor feigned to cast his worser part away
In idle singing for an empty day.

"I have beheld him tremble oft enough
At things he could not choose but trust to me,
Although he knew the world was wise and rough:
And never did he fail to let me see
His love, – his folly and faithlessness, maybe;
And still in turn I gave him voice to pray
Such prayers as cling about an empty day.

"Thou, keen-eyed, reading me, mayst read him through,
For surely little is there left behind;
No power great deeds unnameable to do;
No knowledge for which words he may not find,
No love of things as vague as autumn wind –
– Earth of the earth lies hidden by my clay,
The idle singer of an empty day!

"Children we twain are, saith he, late made wise
In love, but in all else most childish still,
And seeking still the pleasure of our eyes,
And what our ears with sweetest sounds may fill;
Not fearing Love, lest these things he should kill;
Howe'er his pain by pleasure doth he lay,
Making a strange tale of an empty day.

"Death have we hated, knowing not what it meant;
Life have we loved, through green leaf and through sere,
Though still the less we knew of its intent:
The Earth and Heaven through countless year on year,
Slow changing, were to us but curtains fair,
Hung round about a little room, where play
Weeping and laughter of man's empty day.

"O Master, if thine heart could love us yet,
Spite of things left undone, and wrongly done,
Some place in loving hearts then should we get,
For thou, sweet-souled, didst never stand alone,
But knew'st the joy and woe of many an one –

– By lovers dead, who live through thee, we pray,
Help thou us singers of an empty day!"

Fearest thou, Book, what answer thou mayst gain
Lest he should scorn thee, and thereof thou die?
Nay, it shall not be. – Thou mayst toil in vain,
And never draw the House of Fame anigh;
Yet he and his shall know whereof we cry,
Shall call it not ill done to strive to lay
The ghosts that crowd about life's empty day.

Then let the others go! and if indeed
In some old garden thou and I have wrought,
And made fresh flowers spring up from hoarded seed,
And fragrance of old days and deeds have brought
Back to folk weary; and all was not for nought.
– No little part it was for me to play –
The idle singer of an empty day.

This is the title given by May Morris to a group of previously unpublished poems, some of which (in revised form) she included in Volume XXIV of her edition of her father's works, *The Collected Works of William Morris*, 1910-15. In the British Museum manuscript collection they are described as 'Short Poems and Sonnets'. Thematically they relate to *The Earthly Paradise* itself. They show Morris's control of a variety of forms: the octosyllabic couplet ('Hapless Love'), the sonnet ('Written in a copy of *The Earthly Paradise*'; 'Sad-Eyed and Soft and Grey'; 'Rhyme Slayeth Shame'; 'May Grown a-Cold', which is more dramatic than the 'May' sonnet of *The Earthly Paradise*; 'As This Thin Thread'); the tercet ('Fair Weather and Foul'); the rhyming decasyllabic quatrain ('Why Dost Thou Struggle?' – this poem is unfinished); the five-line stanza with modifications of the fifth line ('Our Hands Have Met'); and the rhyming hexameter quatrain ('O Far Away to Seek').

Hapless Love

HIC

Why do you sadly go alone,
O fair friend? Are your pigeons flown,
Or has the thunder killed your bees,
Or he-goats barked your apple-trees?
Or has the red-eared bull gone mad,
Or the mead turned from good to bad?
Or did you find the merchant lied
About the gay cloth scarlet-dyed?
And did he sell you brass for gold,
Or is there murrain in the fold?

ILLE

Nay, no such thing has come to me.
In bird and beast and field and tree,
And all the things that make my store,
Am I as rich as e'er before;
And no beguilers have I known

But Love and Death; and Love is gone,
Therefore am I far more than sad,
And no more know good things from bad.

HIC

Woe worth the while! Yet coming days
May bring another, good to praise.

ILLE

Nay, never will I love again,
For loving is but joyful pain
If all be at its very best;
A rose-hung bower of all unrest;
But when at last things go awry,
What tongue can tell its misery?
And soon or late shall this befall –
The Gods send death upon us all.

HIC

Nay, then, but tell me how she died,
And how it did to thee betide
To love her; for the wise men say
To talk of grief drives grief away.

ILLE

Alas, O friend, it happed to me
To see her passing daintily
Before my homestead day by day –
Would she had gone some other way!
For one day, as she rested there
Beneath the long-leaved chestnuts fair,
In very midst of mid-day heat,
I cast myself before her feet,
And prayed for pity and for love.
How could I dream that words could move
A woman? Soft she looked at me:
"Thou sayest that I a queen should be,"

106

She answered with a gathering smile;
"Well, I will wait a little while;
Perchance the Gods thy will have heard."

And even with that latest word,
The clash of arms we heard anigh;
And from the wood rode presently
A fair knight well apparelled.

And even as she turned her head,
He shortened rein, and cried aloud:
"O beautiful, among the crowd
Of queens thou art the queen of all!"

But when she let her eyelids fall,
And blushed for pleasure and for shame,
Then quickly to her feet he came,
And said, "Thou shalt be queen indeed;
For many a man this day shall bleed
Because of me, and leave me king
Ere noontide fall to evening."

Then on his horse he set the maid
Before him, and no word she said
Clear unto me, but murmuring
Beneath her breath some gentle thing,
She clung unto him lovingly;
Nor took they any heed of me.

Through shade and sunlight on they rode
But 'neath the green boughs I abode,
Nor noted aught that might betide.
The sun waned and the shade spread wide;
The birds came twittering overhead;
But there I lay as one long dead.

But ere the sunset, came a rout
Of men-at-arms with song and shout,
And bands of lusty archers tall,
And spearmen marching like a wall,
Their banners hanging heavily,
That no man might their blazon see;
And ere their last noise died away,
I heard the clamour of the fray
That swelled and died and rose again;
Yet still I brooded o'er my pain
Until the red sun nigh was set,
And then methought I e'en might get
The rest I sought, nor wake forlorn
Midst fellow-men the morrow morn;
So forth I went unto the field,
One man without a sword or shield.
But none was there to give me rest,
Tried was it who was worst and best,
And slain men lay on every side;
For flight and chase were turned aside,
And all men got on toward the sea.
But as I went right heavily
I saw how close beside the way
Over a knight a woman lay
Lamenting, and I knew in sooth
My love, and drew a-near for ruth.

There lay the knight who would be king
Dead slain before the evening,
And ever my love cried out and said,
"O sweet, in one hour art thou dead
And I am but a maiden still!
The Gods this day have had their will
Of thee and me; whom all these years
They kept apart: that now with tears
And blood and bitter misery
Our parting and our death might be."

Then did she rise and look around,
And took his drawn sword from the ground
And on its bitter point she fell –
No more, no more, O friend, to tell!
No more about my life, O friend!
One course it shall have to the end.

O Love, come from the shadowy shore,
And by my homestead as before
Go by with sunlight on thy feet!
Come back, if but to mock me, sweet!

HIC

O fool! what love of thine was this,
Who never gave thee any kiss,
Nor would have wept if thou hadst died?
Go now, behold the world is wide:
Soon shalt thou find some dainty maid
To sit with in thy chestnut shade,
To rear fair children up for thee,
As those few days pass silently,
Uncounted, that may yet remain
'Twixt thee and that last certain pain.

ILLE

Art thou a God? Nay, if thou wert,
Wouldst thou belike know of my hurt,
And what might sting and what might heal?
The world goes by 'twixt woe and weal
And heeds me not; I sit apart
Amid old memories. To my heart
My love and sorrow must I press;
It knoweth its own bitterness.

Written in a copy of The Earthly Paradise, *Dec. 25, 1870*

So many stories written here
And none among them but doth bear
Its weight of trouble and of woe!
Well may you ask why it is so;
For surely neither sour nor dull
In such a world, of fair things full,
Should folk be.

             Ah, my dears, indeed
My wisdom fails me at my need
To tell why tales that move the earth
Are seldom of content and mirth.
Yet think if it may come of this –
That lives fulfilled of ease and bliss
Crave not for aught that we can give,
And scorn the broken lives we live;
Unlike to us they pass us by,
A dying laugh their history.
But those that struggled sore, and failed
Had one thing left them, that availed
When all things else were nought –

                E'en Love –
Whose sweet voice, crying as they strove,
Begat sweet pity, and more love still,
Waste places with sweet tales to fill;
Whereby we, living here, may learn
Our eyes toward very Love to turn,
And all the pain it bringeth meet
As nothing strange amid the sweet:
Whereby we too may hope to be
Grains in the great world's memory
Of pain endured, and nobleness
That life ill-understood doth bless.

Words over-grave and sad for you
Maybe: but rime will still be true
Unto my heart – most true herein
In wishing, dear hearts, you may win
A life of every ill so clear,
That little tale for folk to hear
It may be: yet so full of love,
That e'en these words your hearts may move,
Years and years hence, when unto me
Life is a waste and windless Sea.

Sad-eyed and Soft and Grey

Sad-eyed and soft and grey thou art, O morn!
  Across the long grass of the marshy plain
  Thy west wind whispers of the coming rain,
Thy lark forgets that May is grown forlorn
Above the lush blades of the springing corn,
  Thy thrush within the high elm strives in vain
  To store up tales of spring for summer's pain –
Vain day, why wert thou from the dark night born?

O many-voiced strange morn, why must thou break
  With vain desire the softness of my dream
  Where she and I alone on earth did seem?
How hadst thou heart from me that land to take
Wherein she wandered softly for my sake
  And I and she no harm of love might deem?

Rhyme Slayeth Shame

If as I come unto her she might hear,
  If words might reach her when from her I go,
  Then speech a little of my heart might show,
Because indeed nor joy nor grief nor fear
Silence my love; but her gray eyes and clear,
  Truer than truth, pierce through my weal and woe;
  The world fades with its woods, and naught I know
But that my changed life to My Life is near.

Go, then, poor rhymes, who know my heart indeed,
    And sing to her the words I cannot say, –
    That Love has slain Time, and knows no today
And no tomorrow; tell her of my need,
And how I follow where her footsteps lead,
    Until the veil of speech death draws away.

May Grown a-Cold

O certainly, no month this is but May!
  Sweet earth and sky, sweet birds of happy song,
  Do make thee happy now, and thou art strong,
And many a tear thy love shall wipe away
And make the dark night merrier than the day,
  Straighten the crooked paths and right the wrong,
  And tangle bliss so that it tarry long.
Go cry aloud the hope the Heavens do say!

Nay what is this? and wherefore lingerest thou?
    Why sayest thou the sky is hard as stone?
    Why sayest thou the thrushes sob and moan?
Why sayest thou the east tears bloom and bough?
Why seem the sons of man so hopeless now?
    Thy love is gone, poor wretch, thou art alone!

As this Thin Thread

As this thin thread upon thy neck shall lie
　So on thy heart let my poor love abide
　Not noted much, and yet not cast aside;
　For it may be that fear and mockery
And shame, earth's tyrants, the thin thing shall try
　Nor scorch therefrom what little worth may hide
　Amidst its pettiness, till fully tried
Time leaves it as a thing that will not die.

Then hearken! thou who forgest day by day
　No chain, but armour that I needs must wear
　Although at whiles I deem it hard to bear,
If thou to thine own work no hand will lay,
That which I took I may not cast away,
　Keep what I give till Death our eyes shall clear.

Fair Weather and Foul

Speak nought, move not, but listen, the sky is full of gold,
No ripple on the river, no stir in field or fold,
All gleams but nought doth glisten, but the far-off unseen sea.

Forget days past, heart broken, put all thy memory by!
No grief on the green hill-side, no pity in the sky,
Joy that may not be spoken fills mead and flower and tree.

Look not, they will not heed thee, speak not, they will not hear,
Pray not, they have no bounty, curse not, they may not fear,
Cower down, they will not heed thee; long-lived the world shall
　　be.

Hang down thine head and hearken, for the bright eve mocks
    thee still
Night trippeth on the twilight, but the summer hath no will
For woes of thine to darken, and the moon hath left the sea.

Hope not to tell thy story in the rest of grey-eyed morn,
In the dawn grown grey and rainy, for the thrush ere day is born
Shall be singing to the glory of the day-star mocking thee.

Be silent, worn and weary, till their tyranny is past,
For the summer joy shall darken, and the wind wail low at last,
And the drifting rack and dreary shall be kind to hear and see.

Thou shalt remember sorrow, thou shalt tell all thy tale
When the rain fills up the valley, and the trees amid their wail
Think far beyond tomorrow, and the sun that yet shall be.

Hill-side and vineyard hidden, and the river running rough,
Toward the flood that meets the northlands, shall be rest for thee
    enough
For thy tears to fall unbidden, for thy memory to go free.

Rest then, when all moans round thee, and no fair sunlitten lie
Maketh light of sorrow underneath a brazen sky,
And the tuneful woe hath found thee, over land and over sea.

Why Dost Thou Struggle

Why dost thou struggle, strive for victory
Over my heart that loveth thine so well?
When Death shall one day have its will of thee
And to deaf ears thy triumph thou must tell.

Unto deaf ears or unto such as know
The hearts of dead and living wilt thou say:

114

A childish heart there loved me once, and lo
I took his love and cast his love away.

A childish greedy heart! yet still he clung
So close to me that much he pleased my pride
And soothed a sorrow that about me hung
With glimpses of his love unsatisfied –

And soothed my sorrow – but time soothed it too
Though ever did its aching fill my heart
To which the foolish child still closer drew
Thinking in all I was to have a part.

But now my heart grown silent of its grief
Saw more than kindness in his hungry eyes:
But I must wear a mask of false belief
And feign that nought I knew his miseries.

I wore a mask, because though certainly
I loved him not, yet was there something soft
And sweet to have him ever loving me:
Belike it is I well-nigh loved him oft –

Nigh loved him oft, and needs must grant to him
Some kindness out of all he asked of me
And hoped his love would still hang vague and dim
About my life like half-heard melody.

He knew my heart and over-well knew this
And strove, poor soul, to pleasure me herein;
But yet what might he do some doubtful kiss
Some word, some look might give him hope to win.

Poor hope, poor soul, for he again would come
Thinking to gain yet one more golden step
Toward Love's shrine, and lo the kind speech dumb
The kind look gone, no love upon my lip –

Yea gone, yet not my fault, I knew of love
But my love and not his; how could I tell
That such blind passion in him I should move?
Behold I have loved faithfully and well;

Love of my love so deep and measureless
O lords of the new world this too ye know ...

Our Hands Have Met

Our hands have met, our lips have met,
Our souls – who knows when the wind blows
How light souls drift mid longings set,
If thou forget'st, can I forget
The time that was not long ago?

Thou wert not silent then, but told
Sweet secrets dear – I drew so near
Thy shamefaced cheeks grown overbold,
That scarce thine eyes might I behold!
Ah was it then so long ago!

Trembled my lips and thou wouldst turn
But hadst no heart to draw apart,
Beneath my lips thy cheek did burn –
Yet no rebuke that I might learn;
Yea kind looks still, not long ago.

Wilt thou be glad upon the day
When unto me this love shall be
An idle fancy passed away,
And we shall meet and smile [and] say
"O wasted sighs of long ago!"

Wilt thou rejoice that thou hast set
Cold words, dull shows 'twixt hearts drawn close,
That cold at heart I live on yet,
Forgetting still that I forget
The priceless days of long ago?

O Far Away to Seek

O far away to seek, Close-hid for heart to find,
O hard to cast away, Impossible to bind!
A pain when sought and found, A pain when slipped away,
Yet by whatever name, Be nigh us, Love, today.

Sweet was the summer day, Before thou camest here,
But never sweet to me, And Death was drawing near!
Is it summer still? What meaneth the word Death,
What meaneth all the joy Thy mouth, Love, promiseth?

Wherefore must thou babble Of thy finding me alone?
What is this idle word, That thou may'st yet be gone?
Laugh, laugh, Love, as I laugh, When mine own love kisseth me
And saith no more of bliss Twixt lips and lips shall be.

O Love, thou hast slain time, How shall he live again?
We bless thy bitter wound, We bless thy sleepless pain –
Hope and fear slain each of each Doubt forgetting all he said
Death in some place forgotten Lingering, and half dead.

When my hand forgets her cunning I will loose thee, Love, and
    pray
– Ah and pray to what – For a never-ending day,
Where we may sit apart, Hapless, undying still,
With thoughts of the old story Our sundered hearts to fill.

LOVE IS ENOUGH
1872

This is Morris's most structurally complex poem, and perhaps for this reason it has never achieved popularity. At its centre is the morality-play of King Pharamond and his search for love, which is acted before a newly-wedded Emperor and Empress in an unspecific medieval world. What is included here is the recurring element called 'The Music', written in a fluent rhymed stanza, perhaps to be sung (though the work was never performed in Morris's lifetime). These passages occur at important moments in the story and provide an atmospheric effect:

(i) The first occurs at the entrance of the Emperor and Empress;

(ii) the second as the singers enter and stand before the curtain before the play begins;

(iii) the third comes at the end of what may be seen as the first act of the play 'Of Pharamond the Freed', when the King, who is weighed down by a mysterious sorrow, calls on his counsellor Oliver to accompany him in search of 'some opening...In the clouds that cling round me;'

(iv) the fourth is at the end of the second act when Pharamond is about to set off in search of his beloved;

(v) the fifth concludes Act Three, with Pharamond and Oliver benighted in a yew-wood;

(vi) the sixth ends the short Act Four, as Oliver pronounces a lengthy speech over the body of the sleeping Pharamond, calling on God to help them to find their way out of the misty valley. In the fifth act, 'Music with singing' is heard as Love finally comes to Pharamond and brings to him the beloved, Azalais;

(vii) the seventh passage follows the mutual recognition of the lovers;

(viii) the eighth concludes the sixth act, in which Pharamond leaves the Kingship to Theobald and Honorius, and sets off for the 'poor land and Kingless' where his love awaits his return: it is the most affirmative of the group, its last four lines taking the reader into an allegorical landscape of fulfilment and healing, and concluding with the confident 'Cry out! for he heedeth, fair Love that led home.' The frame poem moves on to an epilogue and a finale.

LOVE IS ENOUGH: though the World be a-waning
And the woods have no voice but the voice of complaining,
   Though the sky be too dark for dim eyes to discover
The gold-cups and daisies fair blooming thereunder,
Though the hills be held shadows, and the sea a dark wonder,
   And this day draw a veil over all deeds passed over,
Yet their hands shall not tremble, their feet shall not falter;
The void shall not weary, the fear shall not alter
   These lips and these eyes of the loved and the lover.

LOVE IS ENOUGH: have no thought for to-morrow
   If ye lie down this even in rest from your pain,
Ye who have paid for your bliss with great sorrow:
   For as it was once so it shall be again.
   Ye shall cry out for death as ye stretch forth in vain

Feeble hands to the hands that would help but they may not,
   Cry out to deaf ears that would hear if they could;
Till again shall the change come, and words your lips say not
   Your hearts make all plain in the best wise they would
   And the world ye thought waning is glorious and good:

And no morning now mocks you and no nightfall is weary,
   The plains are not empty of song and of deed:
The sea strayeth not, nor the mountains are dreary;
   The wind is not helpless for any man's need,
   Nor falleth the rain but for thistle and weed.

O surely this morning all sorrow is hidden,
   All battle is hushed for this even at least;
And no one this noontide may hunger, unbidden
   To the flowers and the singing and the joy of your feast
   Where silent ye sit midst the world's tale increased.

Lo, the lovers unloved that draw nigh for your blessing!
   For your tale makes the dreaming whereby yet they live
The dreams of the day with their hopes of redressing,
   The dreams of the night with the kisses they give,
   The dreams of the dawn wherein death and hope strive.

Ah, what shall we say then, but that earth threatened often
   Shall live on for ever that such things may be,
That the dry seed shall quicken, the hard earth shall soften,
   And the spring-bearing birds flutter north o'er the sea,
   That earth's garden may bloom round my love's feet and me?

(iii)

LOVE IS ENOUGH: it grew up without heeding
   In the days when ye knew not its name nor its measure,
   And its leaflets untrodden by the light feet of pleasure
Had no boast of the blossom, no sign of the seeding,
   As the morning and evening passed over its treasure.

And what do ye say then? – That Spring long departed
   Has brought forth no child to the softness and showers;
– That we slept, and we dreamed through the Summer of flowers;
We dreamed of the Winter, and waking dead-hearted
   Found Winter upon us and waste of dull hours.

Nay, Spring was o'er-happy and knew not the reason,
   And Summer dreamed sadly, for she thought all was ended
   In her fulness of wealth that might not be amended;
But this is the harvest and the garnering season,
   And the leaf and the blossom in the ripe fruit are blended.

It sprang without sowing, it grew without heeding,
  Ye knew not its name and ye knew not its measure,
  Ye noted it not mid your hope and your pleasure;
There was pain in its blossom, despair in its seeding,
  But daylong your bosom now nurseth its treasure.

(iv)

LOVE IS ENOUGH: draw near and behold me
  Ye who pass by the way to your rest and your laughter,
  And are full of the hope of the dawn coming after;
For the strong of the world have bought me and sold me
  And my house is all wasted from threshold to rafter.
    – Pass by me, and hearken, and think of me not!

Cry out and come near; for my ears may not hearken,
  And my eyes are grown dim as the eyes of the dying.
  Is this the grey rack o'er the sun's face a-flying?
Or is it your faces his brightness that darken?
Comes a wind from the sea, or is it your sighing?
    – Pass by me and hearken, and pity me not!

Ye know not how void is your hope and your living:
  Depart with your helping lest yet ye undo me!
  Ye know not that at nightfall she draweth near to me,
There is soft speech between us and words of forgiving
  Till in dead of the midnight her kisses thrill through me.
    – Pass by me and hearken, and waken me not!

Wherewith will ye buy it, ye rich who behold me?
  Draw out from your coffers your rest and your laughter,
  And the fair gilded hope of the dawn coming after!
Nay this I sell not, – though ye bought me and sold me, –
  For your house stored with such things from threshold to rafter.
    – Pass by me, I hearken, and think of you not!

121

LOVE IS ENOUGH: through the trouble and tangle
   From yesterday's dawning to yesterday's night
I sought through the vales where the prisoned winds wrangle,
   Till, wearied and bleeding, at end of the light
   I met him, and we wrestled, and great was my might.

O great was my joy, though no rest was around me,
   Though mid wastes of the world were we twain all alone,
For methought that I conquered and he knelt and he crowned me,
   And the driving rain ceased, and the wind ceased to moan,
   And through clefts of the clouds her planet outshone.

O through clefts of the clouds 'gan the world to awaken,
   And the bitter wind piped, and down drifted the rain,
And I was alone – and yet not forsaken,
   For the grass was untrodden except by my pain:
   With a Shadow of the Night had I wrestled in vain.

And the Shadow of the Night and not Love was departed;
   I was sore, I was weary, yet Love lived to seek;
So I scaled the dark mountains, and wandered sad-hearted
   Over wearier wastes, where e'en sunlight was bleak,
   With no rest of the night for my soul waxen weak.

With no rest of the night; for I waked mid a story
   Of a land wherein Love is the light and the lord,
Where my tale shall be heard, and my wounds gain a glory,
   And my tears be a treasure to add to the hoard
   Of pleasure laid up for his people's reward.

Ah, pleasure laid up! haste thou onward and listen,
   For the wind of the waste has no music like this,
And not thus do the rocks of the wilderness glisten:
   With the host of his faithful through sorrow and bliss
   My Lord goeth forth now, and knows me for his.

LOVE IS ENOUGH: cherish life that abideth,
 Lest ye die ere ye know him, and curse and misname him;
 For who knows in what ruin of all hope he hideth,
On what wings of the terror of darkness he rideth?
 And what is the joy of man's life that ye blame him
  For his bliss grown a sword, and his rest grown a fire?

Ye who tremble for death, or the death of desire,
 Pass about the cold winter-tide garden and ponder
On the rose in his glory amidst of June's fire,
 On the languor of noontide that gathered the thunder,
 On the morn and its freshness, the eve and its wonder:
  Ye may wake it no more – shall Spring come to awaken?

Live on, for Love liveth, and earth shall be shaken
 By the wind of his wings on the triumphing morning,
When the dead, and their deeds that die not shall awaken,
 And the world's tale shall sound in your trumpet of warning,
 And the sun smite the banner called Storm of the Scorning,
  And dead pain ye shall trample, dead fruitless desire,
  As ye went to pluck out the new world from the fire.

LOVE IS ENOUGH: while ye deemed him a-sleeping,
 There were signs of his coming and sounds of his feet;
 His touch it was that would bring you to weeping,
 When the summer was deepest and music most sweet:
 In his footsteps ye followed the day to its dying,
 Ye went forth by his gown-skirts the morning to meet:
 In his place on the beaten-down orchard-grass lying,
 Of the sweet ways ye pondered left for life's trying.

Ah, what was all dreaming of pleasure anear you,
  To the time when his eyes on your wistful eyes turned,
And ye saw his lips move, and his head bend to hear you,
  As new-born and glad to his kindness ye yearned?
    Ah, what was all dreaming of anguish and sorrow,
  To the time when the world in his torment was burned,
    And no god your heart from its prison might borrow,
    And no rest was left, no today, no tomorrow?

All wonder of pleasure, all doubt of desire,
  All blindness, are ended, and no more ye feel
If your feet tread his flowers or the flames of his fire,
  If your breast meet his balms or the edge of his steel.
    Change is come, and past over, no more strife, no more
      learning:
  Now your lips and your forehead are sealed with his seal,
    Look backward and smile at the thorns and the burning.
    – Sweet rest, O my soul, and no fear of returning!

(viii)

LOVE IS ENOUGH: ho ye who seek saving,
  Go no further; come hither; there have been who have found it,
And these know the House of Fulfilment of Craving;
  These know the Cup with the roses around it;
  These know the World's Wound and the balm that hath bound it:
Cry out, the World heedeth not, 'Love, lead us home!'

He leadeth, He hearkeneth, He cometh to you-ward;
  Set your faces as steel to the fears that assemble
Round his goad for the faint, and his scourge for the froward,
  Lo his lips, how with tales of last kisses they tremble!
  Lo his eyes of all sorrow that may not dissemble!
Cry out, for he heedeth, 'O Love, lead us home!'

O hearken the words of his voice of compassion:
   'Come cling round about me, ye faithful who sicken
Of the weary unrest and the world's passing fashion!
   As the rain in mid-morning your troubles shall thicken,
   But surely within you some Godhead doth quicken,
As ye cry to me heeding, and leading you home.

'Come – pain ye shall have, and be blind to the ending!
   Come – fear ye shall have, mid the sky's overcasting!
Come – change ye shall have, for far are ye wending!
   Come – no crown ye shall have for your thirst and your fasting,
   But the kissed lips of Love and fair life everlasting!
Cry out, for one heedeth, who leadeth you home!'

Is he gone? was he with us? – ho ye who seek saving,
   Go no further; come hither; for have we not found it?
Here is the House of Fulfilment of Craving;
   Here is the Cup with the roses around it;
   The World's Wound well healed, and the balm that hath bound it:
Cry out! for he heedeth, fair Love that led home.

POEMS BY THE WAY
1891

Morris's final volume of poetry is a collection of various kinds of poems written over a long period, some between 1868 and 1874, others from 1884 onwards. They are here arranged chronologically. The early poems 'Love Fulfilled' and 'Thunder in the Garden' are unusual among Morris's lyrics for their celebratory note, while 'To the Muse of the North', 'Iceland First Seen' and 'Gunnar's Howe' represent Morris's enthusiasm for the Icelandic and Nordic, and show the effect of this on his poetic style, especially the diction.

The later group begins with two sections from 'The Pilgrims of Hope', the narrative poem about the Paris Commune of 1848 which Morris published in *The Commonweal* in 1885. 'The Message of the March Wind' was the introductory section, in which the lovers in the English country-side become aware of the Wind's message about the squalor and exploitation of the city, and although they pass into the security of the inn, the idea of 'tomorrow's uprising to deeds' – the noun suggesting both getting up and insurgency – ends the poem affirmatively. 'Mother and Son' is a monologue in twelve-syllable rhyming couplets in which a mother addresses her baby, recalling their leaving the country to come to London, contrasting her love-match with the prevailing mercenary nature of marriage in a money-dominated society, and hoping that the child will play its part in bringing about a better world. In similar mood are the *Chants for Socialists* which Morris wrote for the Socialist League, three of which are included here, 'The Voice of Toil', 'All for the Cause', and 'A Death Song'. The last was written for the funeral of Alfred Linnell, who died as a result of injuries sustained when he was ridden down by the militia who were breaking up the free-speech demonstration in Trafalgar Square on 13 November 1887, which became known as 'Bloody Sunday'.

A group of poems written between 1885 and 1887 as inscriptions for tapestries designed for Morris and Company by Burne-Jones includes 'Pomona', 'Flora', 'The Orchard' and 'Tapestry Trees' included here. By contrast two late political poems are the translation 'Mine and Thine' of 1889, and the lively ballad in octosyllabic couplets, 'The Folk-Mote by the River'.

The selection concludes with the inscription Morris wrote for the embroidered valance for his own bed at Kelmscott Manor, designed by his daughter May.

Love Fulfilled

Hast thou longed through weary days
For the sight of one loved face?
Hast thou cried aloud for rest,
Mid the pain of sundering hours;
Cried aloud for sleep and death,
Since the sweet unhoped for best
Was a shadow and a breath?
O, long now, for no fear lowers
O'er these faint feet-kissing flowers.
O, rest now; and yet in sleep
All thy longing shalt thou keep.

Thou shalt rest and have no fear
Of a dull awaking near,
Of a life for ever blind,
Uncontent and waste and wide.
Thou shalt wake and think it sweet
That thy love is near and kind.
Sweeter still for lips to meet;
Sweetest that thine heart doth hide
Longing all unsatisfied
With all longing's answering
Howsoever close ye cling.

Thou rememberest how of old
E'en thy very pain grew cold,
How thou might'st not measure bliss
E'en when eyes and hands drew nigh.
Thou rememberest all regret
For the scarce remembered kiss,
The lost dream of how they met,
Mouths once parched with misery.
Then seemed Love born but to die,
Now unrest, pain, bliss are one,
Love, unhidden and alone.

Thunder in the Garden

When the boughs of the garden hang heavy with rain
And the blackbird reneweth his song,
And the thunder departing yet rolleth again,
I remember the ending of wrong.

When the day that was dusk while his death was aloof
Is ending wide-gleaming and strange
For the clearness of all things beneath the world's roof,
I call back the wild chance and the change.

For once we twain sat through the hot afternoon
While the rain held aloof for a while,
Till she, the soft-clad, for the glory of June
Changed all with the change of her smile.

For her smile was of longing, no longer of glee,
And her fingers, entwined with mine own,
With caresses unquiet sought kindness of me
For the gift that I never had known.

Then down rushed the rain, and the voice of the thunder
Smote dumb all the sound of the street,
And I to myself was grown nought but a wonder,
As she leaned down my kisses to meet.

That she craved for my lips that had craved her so often,
And the hand that had trembled to touch,
That the tears filled her eyes I had hoped not to soften
In this world was a marvel too much.

It was dusk 'mid the thunder, dusk e'en as the night,
When first brake out our love like the storm,
But no night-hour was it, and back came the light
While our hands with each other were warm.

And her smile killed with kisses, came back as at first
As she rose up and led me along,
And out to the garden, where nought was athirst,
And the blackbird renewing his song.

Earth's fragrance went with her, as in the wet grass
Her feet little hidden were set;
She bent down her head, 'neath the roses to pass,
And her arm with the lily was wet.

In the garden we wandered while day waned apace
And the thunder was dying aloof;
Till the moon o'er the minster-wall lifted his face,
And grey gleamed out the lead of the roof.

Then we turned from the blossoms, and cold were they grown
In the trees the wind westering moved;
Till over the threshold back fluttered her gown,
And in the dark house was I loved.

To the Muse of the North

O Muse that swayest the sad Northern Song,
Thy right hand full of smiting and of wrong,
Thy left hand holding pity; and thy breast
Heaving with hope of that so certain rest:
Thou, with the grey eyes kind and unafraid,
The soft lips trembling not, though they have said
The doom of the World and those that dwell therein,
The lips that smile not though thy children win
The fated Love that draws the fated Death.
O, borne adown the fresh stream of thy breath,
Let some word reach my ears and touch my heart,
That, if it may be, I may have a part

In that great sorrow of thy children dead
That vexed the brow and bowed adown the head,
Whitened the hair, made life a wondrous dream,
And death the murmur of a restful stream,
But left no stain upon those souls of thine
Whose greatness through the tangled world doth shine.
O Mother, and Love, and Sister all in one,
Come thou; for sure I am enough alone
That thou thine arms about my heart shouldst throw,
And wrap me in the grief of long ago.

Iceland First Seen

Lo from our loitering ship a new land at last to be seen;
Toothed rocks down the side of the firth on the east guard a weary
    wide lea,
And black slope the hillsides above, striped adown with their
    desolate green:
And a peak rises up on the west from the meeting of cloud and of
    sea,
Foursquare from base unto point like the building of Gods that
    have been,
The last of that waste of the mountains all cloud-wreathed and
    snow-flecked and grey,
And bright with the dawn that began just now at the ending of
    day.

Ah! what came we forth for to see that our hearts are so hot with
    desire?
Is it enough for our rest, the sight of this desolate strand,
And the mountain-waste voiceless as death but for winds that
    may sleep not nor tire?
Why do we long to wend forth through the length and breadth
    of a land,

Dreadful with grinding of ice, and record of scarce hidden fire,
But that there 'mid the grey grassy dales sore scarred by the
ruining streams
Lives the tale of the Northland of old and the undying glory of
dreams?

O land, as some cave by the sea where the treasures of old have
been laid,
The sword it may be of a king whose name was the turning of
fight:
Or the staff of some wise of the world that many things made and
and unmade,
Or the ring of a woman maybe whose woe is grown wealth and
delight.
No wheat and no wine grows above it, no orchard for blossom
and shade;
The few ships that sail by its blackness but deem it the mouth of
a grave;
Yet sure when the world shall awaken, this too shall be mighty
to save.

Or rather, O land, if a marvel it seemeth that men ever sought
Thy wastes for a field and a garden fulfilled of all wonder and
doubt,
And feasted amidst of the winter when the fight of the year had
been fought,
Whose plunder all gathered together was little to babble about;
Cry aloud from thy wastes, O thou land, "Not for this nor for that
was I wrought.
Amid waning of realms and of riches and death of things
worshipped and sure,
I abide here the spouse of a God, and I made and I make and I
endure."

O Queen of the grief without knowledge, of the courage that may
not avail,

Of the longing that may not attain, of the love that shall never forget,

More joy than the gladness of laughter thy voice hath amidst of its wail:

More hope than of pleasure fulfilled amidst of thy blindness is set;

More glorious than gaining of all thine unfaltering hand that shall fail:

For what is the mark on thy brow but the brand that thy Brynhild doth bear?

Lone once, and loved and undone by a love that no ages outwear.

Ah! when thy Balder comes back, and bears from the heart of the Sun

Peace and the healing of pain, and the wisdom that waiteth no more;

And the lilies are laid on thy brow 'mid the crown of the deeds thou hast done;

And the roses spring up by thy feet that the rocks of the wilderness wore:

Ah! when thy Balder comes back and we gather the gains he hath won,

Shall we not linger a little to talk of thy sweetness of old,

Yea, turn back awhile to thy travail whence the Gods stood aloof to behold?

Gunnar's Howe above the House at Lithend

Ye who have come o'er the sea to behold this grey minster of lands,

Whose floor is the tomb of time past, and whose walls by the toil of dead hands

Show pictures amidst of the ruin of deeds that have overpast death,

Stay by this tomb in a tomb to ask of who lieth beneath.

Ah! the world changeth too soon, that ye stand there with unbated
  breath,
As I name him that Gunnar of old, who erst in the haymaking tide
Felt all the land fragrant and fresh, as amidst of the edges he died.
Too swiftly fame fadeth away, if ye tremble not lest once again
The grey mound should open and show him glad-eyed without
  grudging or pain.
Little labour methinks to behold him but the tale-teller laboured
  in vain.

Little labour for ears that may hearken to hear his death-conquering
  song,
Till the heart swells to think of the gladness undying that overcame
  wrong.
O young is the world yet, meseemeth, and the hope of it flourishing
  green,
When the words of a man unremembered so bridge all the days
  that have been.
As we look round about on the land that these nine hundred years
  he hath seen.

Dusk is abroad on the grass of this valley amidst of the hill:
Dusk that shall never be dark till the dawn hard on midnight shall
  fill
The trench under Eyiafell's snow, and the grey plain the sea
  meeteth grey.
White, high aloft hangs the moon that no dark night shall brighten
  ere day,
For here day and night toileth the summer lest deedless his time
  pass away.

The Message of the March Wind

Fair now is the spring-tide, now earth lies beholding
With the eyes of a lover, the face of the sun;
Long lasteth the daylight, and hope is enfolding
The green-growing acres with increase begun.

Now sweet, sweet it is through the land to be straying
'Mid the birds and the blossoms and the beasts of the field;
Love mingles with love, and no evil is weighing
On thy heart or mine, where all sorrow is healed.

From township to township, o'er down and by tillage
Fair, far have we wandered and long was the day;
But now cometh eve at the end of the village,
Where over the grey wall the church riseth grey.

There is wind in the twilight; in the white road before us
The straw from the ox-yard is blowing about;
The moon's rim is rising, a star glitters o'er us,
And the vane on the spire-top is swinging in doubt.

Down there dips the highway, toward the bridge crossing over
The brook that runs on to the Thames and the sea.
Draw closer, my sweet, we are lover and lover;
This eve art thou given to gladness and me.

Shall we be glad always? Come closer and hearken:
Three fields further on, as they told me down there,
When the young moon has set, if the March sky should darken,
We might see from the hill-top the great city's glare.

Hark, the wind in the elm-boughs! from London it bloweth,
And telleth of gold, and of hope and unrest;
Of power that helps not; of wisdom that knoweth,
But teacheth not aught of the worst and the best.

Of the rich men it telleth, and strange is the story
How they have, and they hanker, and grip far and wide;
And they live and they die, and the earth and its glory
Has been but a burden they scarce might abide.

Hark! the March wind again of a people is telling;
Of the life that they live there, so haggard and grim,
That if we and our love amidst them had been dwelling
My fondness had faltered, thy beauty grown dim.

This land we have loved in our love and our leisure
For them hangs in heaven, high out of their reach;
The wide hills o'er the sea-plain for them have no pleasure,
The grey homes of their fathers no story to teach.

The singers have sung and the builders have builded,
The painters have fashioned their tales of delight;
For what and for whom hath the world's book been gilded,
When all is for these but the blackness of night?

How long, and for what is their patience abiding?
How oft and how oft shall their story be told,
While the hope that none seeketh in darkness is hiding,
And in grief and in sorrow the world groweth old?

Come back to the inn, love, and the lights and the fire,
And the fiddler's old tune and the shuffling of feet;
For there in a while shall be rest and desire,
And there shall the morrow's uprising be sweet.

Yet, love, as we wend, the wind bloweth behind us,
And beareth the last tale it telleth to-night,
How here in the spring-tide the message shall find us;
For the hope that none seeketh is coming to light.

Like the seed of mid-winter, unheeded, unperished,
Like the autumn-sown wheat 'neath the snow lying green,

Like the love that o'ertook us, unawares and uncherished,
Like the babe 'neath thy girdle that groweth unseen;

So the hope of the people now buddeth and groweth,
Rest fadeth before it, and blindness and fear;
It biddeth us learn all the wisdom it knoweth;
It hath found us and held us, and biddeth us hear:

For it beareth the message: "Rise up on the morrow
And go on your ways toward the doubt and the strife:
Join hope to our hope and blend sorrow with sorrow,
And seek for men's love in the short days of life."

But lo, the old inn, and the lights and the fire,
And the fiddler's old tune and the shuffling of feet;
Soon for us shall be quiet and rest and desire,
And to-morrow's uprising to deeds shall be sweet.

Mother and Son

Now sleeps the land of houses, and dead night holds the street,
And there thou liest, my baby, and sleepest soft and sweet;
My man is away for a while, but safe and alone we lie,
And none heareth thy breath but thy mother, and the moon
    looking down from the sky
On the weary waste of the town, as it looked on the grass-edged
    road
Still warm with yesterday's sun, when I left my old abode,
Hand in hand with my love, that night of all nights in the year;
When the river of love o'erflowed and drowned all doubt and
    fear,
And we too were alone in the world, and once if never again,
We knew of the secret of earth and the tale of its labour and pain.

Lo amidst London I lift thee, and how little and light thou art,
And thou without hope or fear, thou fear and hope of my heart!
Lo here thy body beginning, O son, and thy soul and thy life;
But how will it be if thou livest, and enterest into the strife,
And in love we dwell together when the man is grown in thee,
When thy sweet speech I shall hearken, and yet 'twixt thee and me
Shall rise that wall of distance, that round each one doth grow,
And maketh it hard and bitter each other's thought to know.

Now, therefore, while yet thou art little and hast no thought of
   thine own,
I will tell thee a word of the world; of the hope whence thou hast
   grown,
Of the love that once begat thee, of the sorrow that hath made
Thy little heart of hunger, and thy hands on my bosom laid.
Then mayst thou remember hereafter, as whiles when people say
All this hath happened before in the life of another day;
So mayst thou dimly remember this tale of thy mother's voice,
As oft in the calm of dawning I have heard the birds rejoice,
As oft I have heard the storm-wind go moaning through the
   wood;
And I knew that earth was speaking, and the mother's voice was
   good.

Now, to thee alone will I tell it that thy mother's body is fair,
In the guise of the country maidens who play with the sun and
   the air;
Who have stood in the row of the reapers in the August afternoon,
Who have sat by the frozen water in the high day of the moon,
When the lights of the Christmas feasting were dead in the house
   on the hill,
And the wild geese gone to the salt-marsh had left the winter still.
Yea, I am fair, my firstling; if thou couldst but remember me!
The hair that thy small hand clutcheth is a goodly sight to see;
I am true, but my face is a snare; soft and deep are my eyes,
And they seem for men's beguiling fulfilled with the dreams of
   the wise.

137

Kind are my lips, and they look as though my soul had learned
Deep things I have never heard of. My face and my hands are
     burned
By the lovely sun of the acres; three months of London town
And thy birth-bed have bleached them indeed, "But lo, where
     the edge of the gown"
(So said thy father) "is parting the wrist that is white as the curd
From the brown of the hand that I love, bright as the wing of a
     bird."

Such is thy mother, O firstling, yet strong as the maidens of old,
Whose spears and whose swords were the warders of homestead,
     of field, and of fold.
Oft were my feet on the highway, often they wearied the grass;
From dusk unto dusk of the summer three times in a week would
     I pass
To the downs from the house on the river through the waves of
     the blossoming corn.
Fair then I lay down in the even, and fresh I arose on the morn,
And scarce in the noon was I weary. Ah, son, in the days of thy
     strife
If thy soul could but harbour a dream of the blossom of my life!
It would be as the sunlit meadows beheld from a tossing sea,
And thy soul should look on a vision of the peace that is to be.

Yet, yet the tears on my cheek! and what is this doth move
My heart to thy heart, beloved, save the flood of yearning love?
For fair and fierce is thy father, and soft and strange are his eyes
That look on the days that shall be with the hope of the brave and
     the wise.
It was many a day that we laughed, as over the meadows we
     walked,
And many a day I hearkened and the pictures came as he talked;
It was many a day that we longed, and we lingered late at eve
Ere speech from speech was sundered, and my hand his hand
     could leave.
Then I wept when I was alone, and I longed till the daylight came;

And down the stairs I stole, and there was our housekeeping
     dame
(No mother of me, the foundling) kindling the fire betimes
Ere the haymakiing folk went forth to the meadows down by the
     limes;
All things I saw at a glance; the quickening fire-tongues leapt
Through the crackling heap of sticks, and the sweet smoke up
     from it crept
And close to the very hearth the low sun flooded the floor,
And the cat and her kittens played in the sun by the open door.
The garden was fair in the morning, and there in the road he stood
Beyond the crimson daisies and the bush of southernwood.
Then side by side together through the grey-walled place we
     went,
And O the fear departed, and the rest and sweet content!

Son, sorrow and wisdom he taught me, and sore I grieved and
     learned
As we twain grew into one; and the heart within me burned
With the very hopes of his heart. Ah, son, it is piteous,
But never again in my life shall I dare to speak to thee thus;
So may these lonely words about thee creep and cling,
These words of the lonely night in the days of our wayfaring.
Many a child of woman to-night is born in the town,
The desert of folly and wrong; and of what and whence are they
     grown?
Many and many an one of wont and use is born;
Prudence begets her thousands; "good is a housekeeper's life,
So shall I sell my body that I may be matron and wife."
"And I shall endure foul wedlock and bear the children of need."
Some are there born of hate, many the children of greed.
"I, I too can be wedded, though thou my love hast got."
"I am fair and hard of heart, and riches shall be my lot."
And all these are the good and the happy, on whom the world
     dawns fair.
O son, when wilt thou learn of those that are born of despair,
As the fabled mud of the Nile that quickens under the sun

With a growth of creeping things, half dead when just begun?
E'en such is the care of Nature that man should never die,
Though she breed of the fools of the earth, and the dregs of the
    city sty.
But thou, O son, O son, of very love wert born,
When our hope fulfilled bred hope, and fear was a folly outworn.

On the eve of the toil and the battle all sorrow and grief we
    weighed,
We hoped and we were not ashamed, we knew and we were not
    afraid.

Now waneth the night and the moon; ah, son, it is piteous
That never again in my life shall I dare to speak to thee thus.
But sure from the wise and the simple shall the mighty come to
    birth;
And fair were my fate, beloved, if I be yet on the earth
When the world is awaken at last, and from mouth to mouth they
    tell
Of thy love and thy deeds and thy valour, and thy hope that
    nought can quell.

The Voice of Toil

I heard men saying, Leave hope and praying,
All days shall be as all have been;
To-day and to-morrow bring fear and sorrow,
The never-ending toil between.

When Earth was younger mid toil and hunger,
In hope we strove, and our hands were strong;
Then great men led us, with words they fed us,
And bade us right the earthly wrong.

Go read in story their deeds and glory,
Their names amidst the nameless dead;
Turn then from lying to us slow-dying
In that good world to which they led;

Where fast and faster our iron master,
The thing we made, for ever drives,
Bids us grind treasure and fashion pleasure
For other hopes and other lives.

Where home is a hovel and dull we grovel,
Forgetting that the world is fair;
Where no babe we cherish, lest its very soul perish;
Where mirth is crime, and love a snare.

Who now shall lead us, what God shall heed us
As we lie in the hell our hands have won?
For us are no rulers but fools and befoolers,
The great are fallen, the wise men gone.

I heard men saying, Leave tears and praying,
The sharp knife heedeth not the sheep;
Are we not stronger than the rich and the wronger,
When day breaks over dreams and sleep?

Come, shoulder to shoulder ere the world grows older!
Help lies in nought but thee and me;
Hope is before us, the long years that bore us
Bore leaders more than men may be.

Let dead hearts tarry and trade and marry,
And trembling nurse their dreams of mirth,
While we the living our lives are giving
To bring the bright new world to birth.

Come, shoulder to shoulder ere Earth grows older!
The Cause spreads over land and sea;
Now the world shaketh, and fear awaketh,
And joy at last for thee and me.

All for the Cause

Hear a word, a word in season, for the day is drawing nigh,
When the Cause shall call upon us, some to live, and some to die!

He that dies shall not die lonely, many an one hath gone before;
He that lives shall bear no burden heavier than the life they bore.

Nothing ancient is their story, e'en but yesterday they bled,
Youngest they of earth's beloved, last of all the valiant dead.

E'en the tidings we are telling was the tale they had to tell,
E'en the hope that our hearts cherish, was the hope for which
they fell.

In the grave where tyrants thrust them, lies their labour and
their pain
But undying from their sorrow springeth up the hope again.

Mourn not therefore, nor lament it, that the world outlives their life;
Voice and vision yet they give us, making strong our hands for
strife.

Some had name, and fame, and honour, learn'd they were, and
wise and strong;
Some were nameless, poor, unlettered, weak in all but grief and
wrong.

Named and nameless all live in us; one and all they lead us yet,
Every pain to count for nothing, every sorrow to forget.

Hearken how they cry, "O happy, happy ye that ye were born
In the sad slow night's departing, in the rising of the morn.

"Fair the crown the Cause hath for you, well to die or well to live
Through the battle, through the tangle, peace to gain or peace
to give."

Ah, it may be! Oft meseemeth, in the days that yet shall be,
When no slave of gold abideth 'twixt the breadth of sea to sea,

Oft, when men and maids are merry, ere the sunlight leaves the
    earth,
And they bless the day beloved, all to short for all their mirth,

Some shall pause awhile and ponder on the bitter days of old,
Ere the toil of strife and battle overthrew the curse of gold;

Then 'twixt lips of loved and lover solemn thoughts of us shall
    rise;
We who once were fools defeated, then shall be the brave and
    wise.

There amidst the world new-builded shall our earthly deeds
    abide,
Though our names be all forgotten, and the tale of how we died.

Life or death then, who shall heed it, what we gain or what we
    lose?
Fair flies life amid the struggle, and the Cause for each shall choose.

Hear a word, a word in season, for the day is drawing nigh,
When the Cause shall call upon us, some to live, and some to die!

A Death Song

What cometh here from west to east awending?
And who are these, the marchers stern and slow?
We bear the message that the rich are sending
Aback to those who bade them wake and know.
Not one, not one, nor thousands must they slay,
But one and all if they would dusk the day.

143

We asked them for a life of toilsome earning,
They bade us bide their leisure for our bread;
We craved to speak to tell our woeful learning:
We come back speechless, bearing back our dead.
Not one, not one, nor thousands must they slay,
But one and all if they would dusk the day.

They will not learn; they have no ears to hearken.
They turn their faces from the eyes of fate;
Their gay-lit halls shut out the skies that darken.
But, lo! this dead man knocking at the gate.
Not one, not one, nor thousands must they slay,
But one and all if they would dusk the day.

Here lies the sign that we shall break our prison;
Amidst the storm he won a prisoner's rest;
But in the cloudy dawn the sun arisen
Brings us our day of work to win the best.
Not one, not one, nor thousands must they slay,
But one and all if they would dusk the day.

Pomona

I am the ancient Apple-Queen,
As once I was so am I now.
For evermore a hope unseen,
Betwixt the blossom and the bough.

Ah, where's the river's hidden Gold!
And where the windy grave of Troy?
Yet come I as I came of old,
From out the heart of Summer's joy.

Flora

I am the handmaid of the earth,
I broider fair her glorious gown,
And deck her on her days of mirth
With many a garland of renown.

And while Earth's little ones are fain
And play about the Mother's hem,
I scatter every gift I gain
From sun and wind to gladden them.

The Woodpecker

I once a King and chief
Now am the tree-bark's thief,
Ever 'twixt trunk and leaf
Chasing the prey.

The Lion

The Beasts that be
In wood and waste,
Now sit and see,
Nor ride nor haste.

Mine and Thine

From a Flemish poem of the fourteenth century

Two words about the world we see,
And nought but Mine and Thine they be.
Ah! might we drive them forth and wide
With us should rest and peace abide;
All free, nought owned of goods and gear,
By men and women though it were.
Common to all all wheat and wine
Over the seas and up the Rhine.
No manslayer then the wide world o'er
When Mine and Thine are known no more.

Yea, God, well counselled for our health,
Gave all this fleeting earthly wealth
A common heritage to all,
That men might feed them therewithal,
And clothe their limbs and shoe their feet
And live a simple life and sweet.
But now so rageth greediness
That each desireth nothing less
Than all the world, and all his own;
And all for him and him alone.

The Folk-Mote by the River

It was up in the morn we rose betimes
From the hall-floor hard by the row of limes.

It was but John the Red and I,
And we were the brethren of Gregory;

And Gregory the Wright was one
Of the valiant men beneath the sun,

146

And what he bade us that we did,
For ne'er he kept his counsel hid.

So out we went, and the clattering latch
Woke up the swallows under the thatch.

It was dark in the porch, but our scythes we felt,
And thrust the whetstone under the belt.

Through the cold garden boughs we went
Where the tumbling roses shed their scent.

Then out a-gates and away we strode
O'er the dewy straws on the dusty road,

And there was the mead by the town-reeve's close
Where the hedge was sweet with the wilding rose.

Then into the mowing grass we went
Ere the very last of the night was spent.

Young was the moon, and he was gone,
So we whet our scythes by the stars alone:

But or ever the long blades felt the hay
Afar in the East the dawn was grey.

Or ever we struck our earliest stroke
The thrush in the hawthorn-bush awoke.

While yet the bloom of the swathe was dim
The blackbird's bill had answered him.

Ere half of the road to the river was shorn
The sunbeam smote the twisted thorn.

Now wide was the way 'twixt the standing grass
For the townsfolk unto the mote to pass,

And so when all our work was done
We sat to breakfast in the sun,

While down in the stream the dragon-fly
'Twixt the quivering rushes flickered by;

And though our knives shone sharp and white
The swift bleak heeded not the sight.

So when the bread was done away
We looked along the new-shorn hay,

And heard the voice of the gathering-horn
Come over the garden and the corn;

For the wind was in the blossoming wheat
And drave the bees in the lime-boughs sweet.

Then loud was the horn's voice drawing near,
And it hid the talk of the prattling weir.

And now was the horn on the pathway wide
That we had shorn to the river-side.

So up we stood, and wide around
We sheared a space by the Elders' Mound;

And at the feet thereof it was
That highest grew the June-tide grass;

And over all the mound it grew
With clover blent, and dark of hue.

But never aught of the Elders' Hay
To rick or barn was borne away.

But it was bound and burned to ash
In the barren close by the reedy plash.

For 'neath that mound the valiant dead
Lay hearkening words of valiance said

When wise men stood on the Elders' Mound,
And the swords were shining bright around.

And now we saw the banners borne
On the first of the way that we had shorn;

So we lay the scythe upon the sward
And girt us to the battle-sword.

For after the banners well we knew
Were the Freemen wending two and two.

There then that highway of the scythe
With many a hue was brave and blythe.

And first below was the Silver Chief
Upon the green was the Golden Sheaf.

And on the next that went by it
The White Hart in the Park did sit.

Then on the red the White Wings flew,
And on the White was the Cloud-fleck blue.

Last went the Anchor of the Wrights
Beside the Ship of the Faring Knights.

Then thronged the folk the June-tide field
With naked sword and painted shield,

Till they came adown to the river-side,
And there by the mound did they abide.

Now when the swords stood thick and white
As the mace reeds stand in the streamless bight,

There rose a man on the mound alone
And over his head was the grey mail done.

When over the new-shorn place of the field
Was nought but the steel hood and the shield.

The face on the mound shone ruddy and hale,
But the hoar hair showed from the hoary mail.

And there rose a hand by the ruddy face
And shook a sword o'er the peopled place.

And there came a voice from the mound and said:
"O sons, the days of my youth are dead,

"And gone are the faces I have known
In the street and the booths of the goodly town.

"O sons, full many a flock have I seen
Feed down this water-girdled green.

"Full many a herd of long-horned neat
Have I see 'twixt water-side and wheat.

"Here by this water-side full oft
Have I heaved the flowery hay aloft.

"And oft this water-side anigh
Have I bowed adown the wheat-stalks high.

"And yet meseems I live and learn
And lore of younglings yet must earn.

"For tell me, children, whose are these
Fair meadows of the June's increase?

"Whose are these flocks and whose the neat,
And whose the acres of the wheat?"

Scarce did we hear his latest word,
On the wide shield so rang the sword.

So rang the sword upon the shield
That the lark was hushed above the field.

Then sank the shouts and again we heard
The old voice come from the hoary beard:

"Yea, whose are yonder gables then,
And whose the holy hearths of men?

"Whose are the prattling children there,
And whose the sunburnt maids and fair?

"Whose thralls are ye, hereby that stand,
Bearing the freeman's sword in hand?"

As glitters the sun in the rain-washed grass,
So in the tossing swords it was;

As the thunder rattles along and adown,
E'en so was the voice of the weaponed town.

And there was the steel of the old man's sword
And there was his hollow voice, and his word:

"Many men, many minds, the old saw saith,
Though hereof ye be sure as death.

"For what spake the herald yestermorn
But this, that ye were thrall-folk born;

"That the lord that owneth all and some
Would send his men to fetch us home

"Betwixt the haysel, and the tide
When they shear the corn in the country-side?

"O children, Who was the lord? ye say,
What prayer to him did our fathers pray?

"Did they hold out hands his gyves to bear?
Did their knees his high hall's pavement wear?

"Is his house built up in heaven aloft?
Doth he make the sun rise oft and oft?

"Doth he hold the rain in his hollow hand?
Hath he cleft this water through the land?

"Or doth he stay the summer-tide,
And make the winter days abide?

"O children, Who is the lord? ye say,
Have we heard his name before to-day?

"O children, if his name I know,
He hight Earl Hugh of the Shivering Low:

"For that herald bore on back and breast
The Black Burg under the Eagle's Nest."

As the voice of the winter wind that tears
At the eaves of the thatch and its emptied ears,

E'en so was the voice of laughter and scorn
By the water-side in the mead new-shorn;

And over the garden and the wheat
Went the voice of women shrilly-sweet.

But now by the hoary elder stood
A carle in raiment red as blood.

Red was his weed and his glaive was white,
And there stood Gregory the Wright.

So he spake in a voice was loud and strong:
"Young is the day though the road is long;

"There is time if we tarry nought at all
For the kiss in the porch and the meat in the hall.

"And safe shall our maidens sit at home,
For the foe by the way we wend must come.

"Through the three Lavers shall we go
And raise them all against the foe.

"Then shall we wend the Downland ways,
And all the shepherd spearmen raise.

"To Cheaping Raynes shall we come adown
And gather the bowmen of the town;

"And Greenstead next we come unto
Wherein are all folk good and true.

"When we come our ways to the Outer Wood
We shall be an host both great and good;

"Yea when we come to the open field
There shall be many under shield.

"And maybe Earl Hugh shall lie alow
And yet to the house of Heaven shall go.

"But we shall dwell in the land we love
And grudge no hallow Heaven above.

"Come ye, who think the time o'er long
Till we have slain the word of wrong!

"Come ye who deem the life of fear
On this last day hath drawn o'er near!

"Come after me upon the road
That leadeth to the Erne's abode."

Down then he leapt from off the mound
And back drew they that were around

Till he was foremost of all those
Betwixt the river and the Close.

And uprose shouts both glad and strong
As followed after all the throng;

And overhead the banners flapped,
As we went on our ways to all that happed.

The fields before the Shivering Low
Of many a grief of manfolk know;

There may the autumn acres tell
Of how men met, and what befell.

The Black Burg under the Eagle's nest
Shall tell the tale as it liketh best.

And sooth it is that the River-land
Lacks many an autumn-gathering hand.

And there are troth-plight maids unwed
Shall deem awhile that love is dead;

And babes there are to men shall grow
Nor ever the face of their fathers know.

And yet in the Land by the River-side
Doth never a thrall or an earl's man bide;

For Hugh the Earl of might and mirth
Hath left the merry days of Earth;

And we live on in the land we love,
And grudge no hallow Heaven above.

For the Bed at Kelmscott

The wind's on the wold
And the night is a-cold,
And Thames runs chill
Twixt mead and hill,
But kind and dear
Is the old house here,
And my heart is warm
Midst winter's harm.
Rest, then and rest,
And think of the best
Twixt summer and spring
When all birds sing
In the town of the tree,
And ye lie in me
And scarce dare move
Lest earth and its love
Should fade away
Ere the full of the day.

I am old and have seen
Many things that have been,
Both grief and peace,
And wane and increase.
No tale I tell
Of ill or well,
But this I say,
Night treadeth on day,
And for worst and best
Right good is rest.

The William Morris Society

The life, work and ideas of William Morris are as important today as they were in his lifetime. The William Morris Society exists to make them as widely known as possible.

The many-sidedness of Morris and the variety of his activities bring together in the Society those who are interested in him as designer, craftsman, businessman, poet, socialist or who admire his robust and generous personality, his creative energy and courage. Morris aimed for a state of affairs in which all might enjoy the potential richness of human life. His thought on how we might live, on creative work, leisure and machinery, on ecology and conservation, on the place of the arts in our lives and their relation to politics, as on much else, remains as challenging now as it was a century ago. He provides a focus for those who deplore the progressive dehumanisation of the world in the twentieth century and who believe, with him, that the trend is not inevitable.

The Society provides information on topics of interest to its members and arranges lectures, visits, exhibitions and other events. It encourages the reprinting of his works and the continued manufacture of his textile and wallpaper designs. It publishes a journal twice a year, free to members, which carries articles across the field of Morris scholarship. It also publishes a quarterly newsletter giving details of its programme, new publications and other matters of interest concerning Morris and his circle. Members are invited to contribute items both to the journal and to the newsletter. The William Morris Society has a world-wide membership and offers the chance to make contact with fellow Morrisians both in Britain and abroad.

Regular events include a Kelmscott Lecture, a birthday party held in March, and visits to exhibitions and such places as the William Morris Gallery, Red House, Kelmscott Manor and Standen. These visits, our tours and our short residential study courses enable members living abroad or outside London to participate in the Society's activities. The Society also has local groups in various parts of Britain and affiliated Societies in the USA and Canada.

For further details, write to: The Hon. Membership Secretary
Kelmscott House
26 Upper Mall
Hammersmith
London W6 9TA